SATISFY OUR SOULS

SATISFY OUR SOULS

a cry from the desert

FRANCES WORTHINGTON

Pleasant Word

A Division of WINEPRESS PUBLISHING

Pleasant Word (a division of WinePress Publishing, PO Box 428, Enumclaw, WA 98022) functions only as book publisher. As such, the ultimate design, content, editorial accuracy, and views expressed or implied in this work are those of the author.

Unless otherwise noted, all Scriptures are taken from the Holy Bible, New International Version, Copyright © 1973, 1978, 1984 by the International Bible Society. Used by permission of Zondervan Publishing House. The "niv" and "New International Version" trademarks are registered in the United States Patent and Trademark Office by International Bible Society.

Scripture references marked nlt are taken from the Holy Bible, New Living Translation, copyright © 1996 by Tyndale Charitable Trust. Used by permission of Tyndale House Publishers, Wheaton, Illinois 60189. All rights reserved.

Spiros Zodhiates et al., eds., The Complete Word Study Dictionary: Old Testament (Chattanooga, TN: amg Publishers, 1992).

James Strong, Strong's Exhaustive Concordance of the Bible (Nashville, TN: Abingdon Press, 1970).

ISBN 13: 978-1-4141-0760-8
ISBN 10: 1-4141-0760-9
Library of Congress Catalog Card Number: 2006904728

DEDICATION

To my husband and two precious girls, who have walked this journey in the desert with me. May we continue to have our souls satisfied by God together.

ABOUT THE AUTHOR

"Even the wilderness will rejoice in those days. **The desert will blossom with flowers.** Yes, there will be an abundance of flowers and singing and joy! The deserts will become as green as the mountains of Lebanon, as lovely as Mount Carmel's pastures and the plain of Sharon. There the LORD will display his glory, the splendor of our God."

—Isaiah 35:1-2 NLT

Hi girls! My name is Frances Worthington and I am so blessed that you have chosen to journey through the desert with me. All of my life I have lived from one event to another. I would take Bible study after Bible study and attend every conference that I could find. But, in the time between "highs," I was living just to survive. God was so gracious to bring me out of that cycle and to give me a life as a "desert flower"—one that could thrive even when everything around was wasting away.

I have begun a ministry called Desert Flower Ministries that is designed to encourage those of us who are tired of living from mountaintops to valleys. Girls, if we are going to reach a lost and dying world, we are going to have to thrive in this life! Christ came to give us life abundantly!

I would love to share my journey with you. I am so blessed to have ministered to ladies of all ages for over 10 years! I am thankful that God has given me the opportunity to minister in the US, Africa, and India. What a great God we serve!

I am married to Jay Worthington, Student Pastor at Crabapple First Baptist Church in Alpharetta, Ga. We have two glorious girls named Anli and Virginia Grace. I am a woman, wife, mother, and lover of Christ just like you! I am honored to have you alongside me as a fellow sojourner through this life.

If you would like to know more about Desert Flower Ministries or myself, please visit **www.desertflowerministries.com**. My passion is to meet you all face to face and share our stories. I look forward to meeting you.

TABLE OF CONTENTS

ACKNOWLEDGMENTS

God has been so gracious to surround my path in the desert with those who have mentored, discipled, and loved me along the way. I could never express how their joy in the journey has impacted my own…but I will try! Thank you to those precious ladies who, each in their own way, have taught me to be a "desert flower"…

Mom, you have shown me how "to bloom where I have been planted." We have been on a wild ride together, but I am so glad I had you by my side. Your blessing is irreplaceable!

Honey, praying with you is one of my very first memories. I consider it an honor to be your namesake. Thank you for pouring your passion for the Lord into me at a young age. I will not depart from it!

Kristen, you are truly a "kindred spirit." Your wisdom and mercy have guided me along this journey in more ways than this short page could describe. I love you!

Cherry Junkins, thank you for taking time to teach Sunday school and lead me to my Father!

Jody, you gave me a foundation to build on for the rest of my journey. Thanks for being a servant to the hundreds of youth in Birmingham! You are an amazing example.

Donna, I am blessed to have been a "little Bible study girl." Your ministry is producing fruit and I am honored to have been a part of it!

Brooke, we have learned about the desert the hard way! Thanks for being there through every tear, smile, laugh, and move. I can't tell you how much I value you and your ministry. You are awesome!

Emily and Kristi, our time in Calloway was a blessing! Thank you for being desert flowers throughout your lives. Life is sweeter knowing you.

Shannon, what a blast to go from college buddies to next door neighbors! I have enjoyed our friendship for the past 12 years and I'm looking forward to a lifetime of memories. Thank you for our prayer sessions that take me to the throne room. I am so blessed to have you in my life.

Nelda and Patsy, thank you for daily pouring into young women's lives. You both were beautiful examples of what the Proverbs 31 woman should look like. Thanks for your discipleship.

Margaret, you were the best "roomie" I could have ever prayed to have. From Auburn to Peru to Washington you have been such an example of what a godly woman should be. I love you, Mrs. Bond!

Amanda, your love for missions continues to challenge me. Thank you for being an oasis for those in the deserts around the world. I love you, Mary Poppins!

Amy, your quiet lovely spirit is precious! Thank you for being an amazing example of diligence and grace. Greywood was such fun together!

Penny, thank you for being a friend in the desert. Your support and encouragement were so valuable.

Nicki, your friendship is one of those gifts from God that I could never live without! You wear your love for God all over you and it is so refreshing to meet someone who is "real." Thank you for embracing God!

Terra, during one of the harshest deserts of my life, you and Dave were there. You were encouraging and supportive and you'll never know how much that has meant.

Paula, I cannot tell you what it has been like traveling this road beside you. Your discernment and faith astound me daily. I will never forget singing praise songs and sharing prayer times in my car in the church parking lot! There are too many memories that have you in them to list! I am blessed.

Rhonda, girl you blow me away! Thanks for being a Miriam and taking up the tambourine to lead others in worship. I won't forget that day in Bible study when the "weight of His glory" fell on us. You have a gift. I have been changed by what God does through your gift. Thank you.

Michele, thank you for being in the trenches of Ladies' Bible study. Thank you for helping me with the leader's guide when I just thought I couldn't write another word! You are a blessing.

Dorothy, you are what I hope to be in Christ. Having someone mentor me has been my dream and God has answered that prayer 100 fold by you. Without you, this study would not have happened. Remember our very first conversation about it at Fish N Mix? God is so good.

Thank you to Sheri, Meredith, Paige, Shelly, Tricia, Diane, Jennifer, Cacee, Allison, Becky, Ginger, Debbie, Beth, Tyler, Tina, Cassondra, Denise, Linda, Amy, the Friendship Sunday school class, and the ladies of Crabapple First Baptist Church for being godly women who have blessed my life.

A special thank you to my pastoral staff for their wisdom, guidance, support, and editing advice. You are growing the kingdom! Thank you for your leadership every day. I am so blessed to attend a church where God's Word is proclaimed and Jesus is lifted high. Thank you.

Thank you to my entire family for loving and supporting whatever God has called me to do. You will never know how precious this family has been to me along this journey. I am surely among the most blessed.

A special thank you to all the ladies who were in the very first sessions of this study! Wow, you guys were troopers. From loose pages to this—what a ride! Thank you for your support and your confirmation. You are precious to me. I loved our "tea parties" just soaking in God's word!

My heartfelt gratitude goes to all the students that we have had the opportunity to serve. You have challenged me daily and blessed my life. Thank you for allowing me to be a part of your lives. I love you all!

Thank you to all of those who have prayed and supported this ministry. God has blessed me by each of you. Though I cannot list everyone who has impacted my life, I sure have tried. If I have forgotten anyone, please fault my head and not my heart. Thank you.

"And now to Him who is able to do immeasurable more than all we ask or imagine, according to His power that is at work within us, to Him be glory in the church and in Christ Jesus throughout all generations for ever and ever! Amen."

—Ephesians 3:20-21

I love you, Jesus!

INTRODUCTION: LIFE IN THE DESERT

Most of my life has been lived in the desert. How is it that we have such great beginnings and then find ourselves years later with our shoes full of sand and our heart dried completely out? That is where I have found myself most of my life—gritty and grumbling. I am an Israelite. Maybe you are one yourself?

But the great thing about the desert is that we can only make it so long without water. Our bodies only last so long and so do our souls. Sooner or later (many times for me it was later) we feel our souls cry out so loudly that we can hardly bear it.

This, my friend, is the cry from the desert. And this is a cry that gets answers from God. We are sending out an SOS to God, and He hears us. He gets the message all right, and it's just the kind of thing He loves to answer.

We can't forget that, like our buddies the Israelites, we are God's precious children. Though we find ourselves out in the middle of nowhere, He can find us and come to us and refresh our weary, stubborn heart.

My heart is refreshed. God has been faithful. And so, my journey now leads me to call out to my buddies in the desert and tell them simply what the God of my refreshment has told me. He will bring you out if you are willing. He will satisfy your soul with all good things (Psalm 90:14) and He will bring you to the place you were meant to dwell – the Promised Land.

You will make it if you are willing to give up your sand spurs for a land of milk and honey. I think that is a pretty great tradeoff. But, my fellow pilgrim, it will take faith, dedication, and a choice to let God grow you into a flower thriving in the desert. For you see, it's in those deserts that God's splendor becomes so evident in our lives.

So, come with me and let's put on our sandals and make our way into the desert where we so often find ourselves. We will learn about our lives there, how we can stop living from highs to lows, and have our SOS call answered by God. Come, let's Satisfy Our Souls!

OUT OF BONDAGE

I am so excited about this journey we are about to take together! This week begins with the plan of salvation. That is where any journey must start. Each day of the week will point to the saving grace of God through His Son, Jesus Christ. He is the only way we can ever hope to be released from the bondage of sin in our lives.

If you are already a Christian, take time this week to think of areas in your life that have you held in bondage. Spend this week releasing those to God. This is a week of beginnings. Enjoy this time to lay your life before Him in anticipation of what He is going to do!

WEEK 1 - DAY 1: THE CRY FROM BONDAGE

As we begin this study, God has put it on my heart that we should start at the very beginning. Many of you who are entering into this study are well-seasoned Christians, but I never want to take for granted the fact that there may be someone who has stumbled onto this study and has never heard the incredible news of Jesus Christ and the beautiful way He changes lives. So as we pack our bags along with the Israelite people, we must also begin the journey at the very start.

Read Exodus 3.

Where were the Israelite people?

_____

_____

_____

What did God hear from them?

_____

_____

_____

Why did they need to cry out to God?

_____

_____

_____

We start today looking at the state of the Israelite people. They are in bondage as slaves to the people of Egypt. But our loving God looked at His chosen people and He heard their cry. We must all start our journey the same way: with a true heart's cry for salvation from our bondage. We must look up to God and agree with Him that we are in an awful mess. We can't do this thing on our own. We are in slavery to ourselves and all the rotten things we do each day that are wrong.

Has there ever been a point in your life when you realized that you were longing to be set free?

_____

_____

_____

If you are a Christian, is there something in your life right now that has you in bondage?

_____

_____

_____

Have you ever looked at your life and known you could never save yourself from the mess you have made?

_____

_____

_____

We must realize at the very beginning of this journey that we are slaves. We are in a mess we just can't get out of. We were born sinners. We all have blown it! Our hearts yearn to be set free from this slavery of sin and live a life of victory. But how do we get out of this mess?

What did the Israelite people do?

_____

_____

_____

The Hebrew word for "cry" is to literally "shriek." They were in agony under the op-pression and they called out in pure desperation to the only One who could save them. When we are in slavery we try to find anything other than God to save us. We look to money to fill us – it doesn't. We look to people and relationships to fill us – they don't. We look to stuff to fill us – it doesn't. We go through life crying out from our deepest core to be saved. But Israel had to realize there was only One who could save them—God.

What was God's reaction to their cry?

_____

_____

_____

Isn't that the best news you have heard? God was concerned about their suffering. He was moved. He is that kind of God. He doesn't sit on His heavenly throne, peek down at us, and laugh at the mess we've made. He doesn't say to Himself, "They got what they deserved." No, God is moved. He cares. His kind of caring means freedom for us.

Right now you may be thinking to yourself that you have never cried out to God to save you from the sin that has you in slavery. Your entire being shrieks from under the weight of your burdened life and the slave driver of sin. Well, there is great news to end with today! You can cry out to God this very day! He will be moved and He cares. And when He moves, He saves.

Take time right now to confess your need of God to Him. Tell Him that you know you cannot do this thing on your own. He cares so much about our cries from bondage that He sent His only Son, Jesus Christ, to die for us to make a way where there was no way. Through each day this week, we will be taking the rest of the journey to being truly saved from captivity. We will discuss the impossible gap of sin, the amazing way through Jesus Christ, and our choice to step in faith. This is a serious decision, and we must take great care to understand where this journey is beginning and where it leads.

Please pray now for God to open our hearts to any things in our lives that are keeping us in slavery. Talk to Him personally now and cry out to the only One who can save us and help us! And take confidence that He will be moved.

WEEK 1 - DAY 2: FACING THE IMPOSSIBLE

Take these first few moments and give them to God. Ask Him to reveal areas of your life that you need to give over to Him today. Pray that He will guide your time in His Word.

Yesterday we talked about the cry of bondage. The Israelite people were in slavery and cried out under the slave drivers for salvation. God heard their cry and He was moved. What wonderful news to have the kind of God who is moved and concerned with our hurts and our needs.

But God not only heard their cry, He did something about it. God saw His chosen people under a terrible yoke and had a plan to deliver them. Take a look...

Read Exodus 13:17-18.

Where are the Israelites?

_____

_____

_____

The Israelites are now leaving Egypt. They have been delivered out of Pharaoh's hand – or so they thought. They moved out of Egypt to the border of the Red Sea and camped there. But Pharaoh is about to change his mind about letting them go and begins to pursue them. Look again...

Read Exodus 14:1-11.

What a terrifying sight for the Israelite people. They had cried out to the Lord, and He had been leading them in the desert to the banks of the Red Sea. Just when things seemed to be going all right, they look up, and there were the Egyptians marching after them!

What did the Israelite people do then?

_____

_____

_____

What was their response to being led out of captivity?

_____

_____

_____

They were ready to turn right back and become slaves again. They were between a sea and a hard place! Isn't that what we all have experienced? We realize the sin that separates us from God is enormous. We look one way and see that the captivity of the life we want to turn from is hot on our trail. We look the other way and see the impossibly perfect, unattainable God. Then we despair. We realize that for what we have done in life, we must surely die in the desert! But this is the kind of situation God just loves! Facing the impossible!

Have you come to the place in your life where you see that there is an impossible gap between the sinful life you are leading and the perfection of a holy God?

If you are there at this time, then please cry out to God and tell Him you realize that there is a huge gap between you and Him. This is a gap that only He can provide a way through. When we are honest with Him, we can position ourselves to see the impossibly perfect way that He is about to provide for us!

What does Moses tell the people? (verses 13-14)

_____

_____

_____

Who is about to bring deliverance?

_____

_____

_____

God is about to do something amazing here! He is about to be the one to open up the way. We can't make the way ourselves because we all are sinful – every one of us.

Read Romans 3:10-12.

Who is righteous before God?

_____

_____

_____

Who has turned to Him on their own?

_____

_____

_____

Who does anything good?

_____

_____

_____

The answer to every one of those questions is NO ONE! So, God must make the way for sinful men to come to Him. The good news is that He did make a way! We will study about the perfect way that God gave us tomorrow.

God hears our cries from captivity. Perhaps you are already a Christian but you have found yourself in a lifestyle of captivity. Maybe you have been living a life completely in rebellion to God. Take some time right now and cry out to God. Tell Him you want to be set free from that life of sin.

WEEK 1 - DAY 3: THE AMAZING WAY

Today let's begin by asking God to prepare our hearts for study. Invite His wisdom and Holy Spirit to invade our time together. Give Him all your cares and troubles as we open His Word.

Read Exodus 14:15-19.

Here we are at the banks of the Red Sea. As we look behind us, the Egyptian army is blazing towards us. In front of us stands the Red Sea! This was the impossible gap that we studied yesterday. It is just like the gap we see in front of each of us as we stand in the presence of a holy God.

What did God want Moses to tell the people to do?

_____

_____

_____

What did God want Moses to do?

_____

_____

_____

God asked Moses, "Why are you crying out to me? Tell the people to go!" God was about to do the impossible and the people needed to be ready to act. Moses is about to stretch out his staff over the sea and divide it right down the center so that the people could walk on dry ground. The amazing answer to a cry of desperation! That is our kind of God. He does more than we could ever think or imagine!

The sin in our lives before a holy and righteous God is the impossible gap. It stands before us like an endless sea in all directions. We look to God and can't begin to imagine how He can save us. But then He moves.

Read Luke 1:68-79.

Who is talking?

_____

_____

_____

Who is he talking about in verses 68-75?

_____

_____

_____

And in verses 76-79?

_____

_____

_____

Here we see Zechariah's song of praise to God. He was John the Baptist's father. He is telling about the imminent birth of Jesus Christ. Read closely what Zechariah says about Jesus.

Please write down everything that describes Jesus in his song.

_____

_____

_____

Did you notice some very key words that would relate to the situation of the Israelites? Name them.

_____

_____

_____

This passage describes Jesus as the One who is the horn of salvation, redemption of His people, salvation from our enemies, and our rescue from the hand of our enemies, that we might serve Him without fear. Isn't that just what we all need to hear?

Facing the impossible gap of the Red Sea, the Israelite people needed to know that God would deliver them. And He did! He had a plan that was way beyond their minds and imaginations. He is the same kind of God today. He hears our cries for salvation and He did the impossible through sending His son Jesus Christ to be the "horn of salvation."

Take time today to rejoice in the fact that Jesus Christ is the amazing Way! Take a few moments to reflect on the difficulties that need Christ's amazing power in your life. Claim that power and walk in faith!

WEEK 1 - DAY 4: A STEP OF FAITH

Let's begin this time today with a heart clean before Him. Take a few moments of your own to talk to God. Ask Him to lead our time together and to give you a new and fresh word from Him.

Read Exodus 14:19-20.

Remember yesterday that we were talking about how God knew that in order to save the Israelite people from their bondage, He would have to make an Amazing Way. We discussed that though He made a temporary way for them through the Red Sea, He has done altogether more for us by making Jesus Christ our perfect, eternal Way. Praise His Name!

Today, we are still standing on the banks. We are about to witness the parting of the Red Sea before our eyes, and then something very unusual happens. Read verse 19.

Who had been leading the people?

_____

_____

_____

What else was leading them?

_____

_____

_____

What happened to them both?

_____

_____

_____

Now, what could the Israelite people be thinking? They are about to walk through the sea on dry ground, but the angel of God and the pillar that had been leading them are no longer in front of them, but behind them. Isn't that sometimes how we feel? Just when we are faced with a huge decision or leap of faith it seems that the guidance we had been counting on God bringing is no longer right out there in front of us. We begin to think that God has deserted us right when we need Him the most. Where is He now? Doesn't He know that I need Him? Why would He leave me?

Read verse 20.

Oh, don't those words calm, soothe, and comfort our anxious souls? They do mine. There have been many times when I have been faced with life-altering decisions, battles, or giant steps of faith that seemed to overcome my whole existence. At those times I just need to know that my pillar has not left me.

Where were the angel and the pillar cloud?

_____

_____

_____

What were they doing for the people?

_____

_____

_____

Oh, glory! Do you see that since God had opened the sea and shown them the way, He just needed them to walk in faith that He was still with them? Not only was He still with them, He was fighting their battle from behind. He had their back, if you will. God is so good to us that when we step out in faith onto the dry ground He has prepared, He will always be with us and protect us.

Did you notice God shed light on His people to show them the way and shed darkness on their enemies behind?

Read John 14:6.

What is Jesus to us?

_____

_____

_____

Yesterday we talked about Jesus being the Amazing Way of God through our sea of sinful ways. Today we see Him as Light of our faith. He is the Light that leads our every step to the Father. Because, you see, no one comes to the Father God except through Jesus. The Israelite people could never have made it across the sea without God parting the waters and without Him lighting their way. Today God provides both through Jesus Christ – both for salvation and for the freedom from bondage. He is the only way to freedom.

Read Exodus 14:22.

And they went through. God has provided the Way and the Light. But He will never force us to walk the path. He gives us the choice to step out in faith. It is our calling, but we can choose to continue to drown in the sea, trying to make the way ourselves. We can fight those battles ourselves in darkness without the Light of our Father who loves us. But remember, it is our choice. He has done His part – will you have the faith to go through? Will it be said of your life – she went through?

Remember, the pillar you think has left you is right there fighting the battles you never even see. He is lighting your path and keeping you safe. Step off those comfortable banks and walk through on dry ground, for the Way is prepared!

Take some time now to ask God to shed His light on the things you are trying to do on your own. Give that up to Him and accept the Way that He has already shown us to victory over our sinful lives. We no longer need to have the yoke of slavery on us. We have a new yoke, and this one is of rest and peace. Step off the banks and let Him light your path to freedom!

WEEK 1 - DAY 5: PRAISE HIM!

Enter your time of study today with a sincere prayer of praise. Get away to a quiet spot and spend time just loving WHO He is and not simply what He does for us. That is true praise, when we just love Him.

Read Exodus 15:1-21.

What is the title in your Bible for this section?

_____

_____

_____

In my Bible, the title is "The Song of Moses and Miriam." It is awesome for me to see that when God did His thing, Moses led the people to praise God – not himself. God had delivered them from the captivity of the Egyptians and divided the Red Sea and closed the sea over the armies behind them. He worked through Moses, yet Moses knew who really did the work. He was ready to turn any praise that he got from the people into a praise song to the True Deliverer – God.

Let's go through some of the praises that Moses sang to the Lord and see if we can gain some insight into the heart of a true believer in praise.

Look at verse 2.

What are the things that Moses says God is to him?

_____

_____

_____

_____

_____

_____

He calls God his strength, his song, and his salvation. He is God. He calls God his salvation. The great news is that God is still our salvation. He is the One who saves us from an eternity in hell, from the strongholds of sin, and ultimately He saves us from ourselves. He is the salvation of the world for all time.

Take time right now to praise God for your salvation. Thank Him for saving you from your sin, your life of rebellion, and strongholds. He has become our salvation – praise Him.

Now, take a look at verses 6-7.

How did God win this victory over Pharaoh?

_____

_____

_____

Would you look back with me into Exodus 14:16?

_____

_____

_____

What does God tell Moses to do?

_____

_____

_____

I think it is so interesting that Moses was the one who physically stretched out his hand over the sea, yet he knows that it was God's hand that "shattered the enemy." The heart of a true servant of praise knows that, if she has been used by God in any way, it was God who always gave the victory.

We have to know that even though we took the step of faith to walk across the Red Sea and accept His salvation from our lives of captivity, we did not save ourselves. So many times in our lives we see God working in us, and we become prideful. We think because we ran across the dry land to the other side that we somehow deserve the praise.

To whom did Moses give all credit? Read the entire song.

Isn't it neat to see a man who could have so easily accepted the praise of the Israelite people for parting the Red Sea and delivering them from bondage, turn and give the glory to God? If you look through the entire song of Moses, you will see that he never even talks about anything he did. It's only about God. That's true praise.

When was the last time that you truly praised God – and did not talk about yourself?

Take a few moments now to talk only about God. Just think only of Him and tell Him what you love most about Him. Remember to not include yourself. Just talk about Him. He loves this stuff because He is worthy!

Now read verses 17-18.

Here Moses is displaying his unwavering faith that God will lead them to the ultimate deliverance – the Promised Land. He is not just convinced that God could be big in this circumstance alone, he is convinced that his God is big enough to do everything He said He would. Oh, if we would believe God is that big in our lives today!

Name something God has done in your life that only He could have done.

_____

_____

_____

Is there something in your life right now that you are not sure God can do?

_____

_____

_____

Let's not simply praise God for what He has done in the past; let's praise Him for what He will do in our futures. He is beyond time and space, and He is already completing the good work He began in you. Finally, let's look at what happens when God's people start to praise Him in verses 20-21.

Who is now leading praise to God?

_____

_____

_____

Who is she leading?

_____

_____

_____

Think back to the beginning of the song. It noted that Moses led the Israelite people in a song of praise to the Lord. Well, now see that Miriam, Aaron and Moses' sister, is leading the women of Israel in song with tambourines.

I find that so encouraging! God can call any of us to praise Him for what He has done in our lives! Ladies, this is a verse meant just for us. Please see that Miriam was so full of praise for her God that she led her own praise service, which led the other women to praise. You never know why God puts hard situations in your life, but when we see His glory through those times—good or bad—we are called to praise Him. And when we exclaim His goodness and His victory in our lives, others will join in too!

That's the kind of woman I want to be. I want to be a Miriam. Let's commit our lives to praising our God no matter what the past or future may hold. He is always the same and He is always good. So grab your tambourines, ladies, and get to praising!

INTO THE DESERT

We will find ourselves journeying deep into the desert this week. We begin to see our deserts and find out what God's purpose for them is in our lives. God calls us into these deserts to teach us and to satisfy us.

Most books today will try to give you keys to getting out of these deserts quickly. They promise to have you living the perfect life in just a few easy steps. But God has a unique purpose for these deserts that He calls us to travel through. Some of us will be called into lifelong deserts, but our testimony is how we live and thrive when our lives aren't perfect.

Take this week to look closely at your own deserts. How are you living in them? What does the world see in your life? Do they see joy in the desert or defeat?

WEEK 2 - DAY 1: A TASTE OF THE DESERT

Today, let's begin our time thanking God for time in His Word. Thank Him that He is faithful to meet with you. Ask Him to change your heart with His words and His love.

Read Exodus 16:1.

Now, ladies, we still have our praise music blaring and our tambourines in hand as we begin to feel a bit thirsty. I mean, how long has it been since we have had some water?

Look back at Exodus 15:22-27.

Where have they come from? Verses 22-23

_____

_____

_____

What did God do there? Verse 25

_____

_____

_____

Then, where did He lead them? Verse 27

_____

_____

_____

What does this place remind you of?

_____

_____

_____

The Israelites have just seen God not only part the Red Sea, but He has now turned bitter water into sweetness. Then, He led them into a time of amazing refreshment in Elim – the beach retreat!

God has really done some amazing things using water – the ultimate refresher. He has parted it, sweetened it, and led them to camp near it. He is showing them something that they will need desperately where they are headed now.

Go back and read Exodus 16:1.

Where are they again?

_____

_____

_____

Oh, can't we all relate to the desert? And don't we always seem to find ourselves there right after our times of Elim?

You see, we are about to enter the cycle in which many Christians today find themselves. Here is the scene for you, and see if you can find yourself there…

It is a wonderful October day. We have just left our kids and husbands with lengthy lists and loving kisses as we head to the latest women's conference. We are speeding along the highway with the praise music blaring and the wind in our faces as we laugh and talk with our beloved sisters in Christ.

We check into our hotels like high school seniors on Spring Break. We are giddy and anxious. The rooms are full of laughter and enthusiastic nods as we show off the newest fashions we bought just for that weekend. What a weekend this will be! We sail off to the mile long lines to get into the Conference Center along with 80,000 other energized women from around the country. We all can't wait to get a charge for our dull and drab lives. We all agree that this is just what we need to get us on track. We are all aching for that spiritual jump-start. And surely this will do it!

Nestled between our very best buddies, we get out our new notebook (just purchased for the weekend, of course) and a pretty pen. We are set for a Word from God. And He provides. He is faithful and we are filled. He has been good. We've sung the greatest praise songs. We've heard from God's Word in a fresh and new way. We have cried over the sin in our lives. We are exhausted, but we are refreshed.

Meet your Elim. These are the times that you have camped out with Him, drinking from the wells of His presence and enjoying the shade of His love. He has led you there to meet with you. It was not an accident that you have these times of amazing refreshment. It is His good pleasure and will to lead you into times where He can just pour Himself all over you. Oh, we crave and need those times, and He loves to supply them.

But the rest of the scene must be told.

By Thursday morning, you still have not quite recovered from the weekend away. Your children woke up sick Monday and you nursed them until today. When you finally took them to the doctor's office, it was full so you had to stand in line for hours at the Urgent Care. You're tired from the sleepless nights you've spent blowing noses and administering cough syrup. And, of course, there was the laundry and dishes that almost met you at the door as you came home. Can your husband not do anything while you are away?

Then you think back to Wednesday night, when you faced the girl who is never satisfied with the way you lead the children's Bible study, and no one seemed nearly as excited to hear about your weekend as you thought they'd be. You have not quite gotten around to the commitments you made while you were at the conference, and that quiet time with God hasn't quite happened yet. Maybe next week you can get it all together…

Meet your Desert of Sin. Yep, that's the way it usually happens. Just when God's presence is so close we think we will surely burst wide open for loving it, we look around and life has happened. The feeling is gone and we are thirsty again. What happened to us?

Read Exodus 16:1 again.

You see, we are in good company. The Israelite people had seen God's presence so clearly as a pillar cloud and they knew that He had not left them. Yet here they were in the Desert of Sin and they weren't one bit happy about it.

Can you name a time when you felt God's presence closely?

_____

_____

_____

Have you had times when life crept back in and you found yourself in the desert?

_____

_____

_____

This is the cycle that most of us, at one time or another, find in our spiritual lives. Personally, I have lived that cycle most of my life. You see, I would live from event to event. I was alive and on fire for a little while. Then before long I was in the desert, craving the waters of Elim again. I was very passionate, yet terribly uncommitted. It was dangerous and defeated living.

Does the above scenario ring true of your life? If so, please know that this is not the way God intends for you to live. There is much more in store for your life than this dry cycle of defeat.

Take time now to talk to God about your spiritual journey up until today. Please be thorough about the areas of your life that have not been under His control. Confess any strongholds that are keeping you from breaking out of the cycle of defeat. Please take this time very seriously. We are about to shine some light onto our lives through God's Word, and we desperately need to seek His face on this journey.

WEEK 2 - DAY 2: THE GRUMBLING BEGINS

Oh, how amazing our God is! He transforms lives and invades our hearts with love and forgiveness. Spend some precious time now with your Father. Thank Him for all He is doing in your life right now. Praise Him.

Read Exodus 16:2-3.

What is the overall feeling of the Israelite people?

_____

_____

_____

Have you had times in your life when you could relate to their feelings?

_____

_____

_____

When was this time and what was going on?

_____

_____

_____

I think that all of us have had times of disappointment. We have had really high expectations of the way this whole Christian experience is supposed to be. We have gotten our ideas of what we wanted to be feeling and experiencing at this point in our Christian walk and we are quite sure this down feeling was NOT it. What went wrong?

Well, look back at what the Israelite people were grumbling about.

Read verses 2-3 again.

Why were they grumbling?

_____

_____

_____

They were grumbling because they were hungry. That seems very simple, but it says so much to us today. We grumble and we complain because we are hungry. And we are hungry because we are not feeding on God's Word. We are living our lives looking around at all of the things that we thought we would have by this time and we start to feel hungry. We want more than this daily life of mediocrity.

What did the people do about their hunger?

_____

_____

_____

They complained. How much like the Israelite people we are! They began to whine to anyone who would listen. They also began to cast blame.

We too want to cast blame. We blame our pastors for not preaching sermons that relate to our lives. We blame our Sunday school teachers for not teaching exciting lessons. We blame the church leaders for not meeting our every need and want. We blame God. Wow, how the grumbling goes! We grumble to the point where we even have a bone to pick with God.

"Oh, if only we had died by the Lord's hand in Egypt!"

Take a moment to digest that statement. Are we so hungry in our own spiritual lives that we begin to wish we had just been left for dead in our bondage? Oh, my heart is literally breaking at that statement because I have felt just that hungry. I just didn't know I was hungry. I just thought that I needed someone to blame. Others were the reason I was in this shape.

Can you relate to the hunger you hear in those words cried out by the people of Israel?

_____

_____

_____

Are you casting blame for your own hunger into other areas of your life?

_____

_____

_____

You see, there is more to this Christian life than grumbling in the desert. There really is! I know this from being a desert dweller. I have been in ministry most of my college and adult life. And truthfully, most of those years I have also lived in the depth of the desert. Not that there weren't Red Sea days and beach retreats in Elim. But those times were always followed by hunger, thirst, and grumbling. I couldn't seem to learn to live and thrive in my times of desert. I couldn't seem to live out what I felt in those times of refreshment. It became nothing more than a high. I couldn't survive in the desert. And it all would begin because I didn't realize my own hunger. We must understand what is really behind all of our blame and grumbling before we can seek to be filled.

Read Luke 4: 1-2.

What was Jesus filled with in these verses?

_____

_____

_____

Where then was He led?

_____

_____

_____

Who led Him to the desert?

_____

_____

_____

What physical condition was he in?

_____

_____

_____

Oh, amazing Word of God! I had actually left this day's work and had lain down to meditate on His goodness. God literally got me up out of bed and led me right to these verses! God wasn't finished with this day yet! Glory to His Name!

Do you see that Jesus had just been baptized and was full of the Holy Spirit? And at that time, that same Holy Spirit led him into the desert to be tempted. He ate nothing for 40 days and nights. Now He was hungry.

Oh, how we just need to know that Jesus has been in that same desert we may be in today. He was hungry. He was tempted. Yet He survived in the desert! And we can too. We just have to be willing to live like His example.

Now read Luke 4:3-4.

What did Satan tempt him to do?

_____

_____

_____

What was Jesus' response?

_____

_____

_____

Let these words dwell in you so richly. Do you see that being in the desert may not be due to fact that there is sin in our lives or that we have gotten off track somewhere along the way? Jesus was led into the desert full of the Holy Spirit on a major God-high. Yet, He gave the prescription for how to be victorious in the desert: depend on God's Word. That is the very heart of what we are going to be digging into these next weeks together.

Never forget that Satan knows we will be led into times of desert. We will have them. That's a given, because Jesus did. So Satan will try to use those times of hunger to shift our focus off God's Word to the things of this earth to satisfy ourselves. He wants us to think that what he can offer will be so much better than the desert. We must stay rooted and grounded in the precious, life–giving Word of God.

Read Luke 4:14.

Now, just dance a few minutes in those words! Jesus was led into the desert by the Holy Spirit, but he left that desert in the power of the Holy Spirit. That is our goal, girls! We are going to learn how to not only make it out of the desert alive, but to live every day in the desert in the full power of the Holy Spirit. Let's see this journey through and claim the power meant for us.

Are you hungry for something more?

_____

_____

_____

We all hunger in some area of our lives. We must start this journey honestly and openly before God. Spend time with Him now just declaring your need. We are needy people. God made us that way. But He didn't make us to live defeated by our blame games and grumbling sessions. There is more. But we have to get to the core—we just need a huge work from Him.

Lay it all out before Him. Declare it openly that you are hungry. Confess your need of His great work in your life right now. Then hang on through this study, because that is just the kind of invitation He is waiting for from you!

WEEK 2 - DAY 3: BLESSINGS AND DOUBTS

Today we will begin with a time of reflection on the blessings God has given you. Please use the space below to recount some of the amazing blessings that God gives His beloved children. This exercise will be the basis for today's lesson together. Please take your time and enjoy what God has done!

_____

_____

Now read Exodus 16:3.

We talked about the grumbling of the people of Israel and that their complaining came from hunger. Today we will look at the second reason they grumbled against Moses and the Lord.

What did they accuse Moses and God of doing to them?

_____

_____

They were literally saying that God had led them out of their bondage to bring them into a horrible death. Think on that a minute. They were calling into question the very nature of God Himself. Wow.

Why do you think they would do something like that?

_____

_____

Has there ever been a time when you have questioned the very character of God?

_____

_____

Doubt can be a powerful temptation while we are in our deserts. It is easy to look around at our circumstances and begin to doubt that this Christian life is really worth the fight. The bondage of Egypt seems to look better and better all the time. We want to return to the land that is comfortable and easy, even if that means more bondage. When we find ourselves coming off the mountaintop experiences and entering into deserts of hunger, we begin to question the very nature of the God who saved us.

The Israelites did that very thing. They really believed at that moment that the same God who heard their cries from slavery would bring them out just to kill them. We may not say those exact words, but we look at our lives and think that God saved us to bind us into a life of boredom, rules, hypocrisy, and defeat! We think, in essence, that God saved us to heaven but is killing us on earth. He has freed us to enter heaven, but bound us to hell on earth.

Have you ever felt like God has saved you and allowed you to enter heaven, but has bound you to a life of misery here on earth?

If so, what has made you feel that way?

_____

_____

What has caused you to doubt the goodness of God?

_____

_____

Read Psalm 63.

Who is this Psalm written by?

_____

_____

Where is he at the time he writes the Psalm?

_____

_____

David wrote this psalm in the Desert of Judah. He was king at the time, and yet he had fled to the desert to escape the overthrow of his son Absalom. Read the story for yourself.

Read 2 Samuel 15.

How did Absalom gain the hearts of the people of Israel?

_____

_____

How did the people feel as David left (verse 23)?

_____

_____

What valley did David cross?

_____

_____

What did he enter after he crossed it?

_____

_____

What did they take with them (verse 24)?

_____

_____

What did David decide to do with it?

_____

_____

Now that you have read part of the story yourself, let's look at the scene a minute. David is the true king of Israel. His son, Absalom, has conspired against him, and David had to give up reigning as king to flee to the desert. He and the people with him made one last sacrifice then returned the Ark of the Covenant to the city where his son was ruling. David begins the ascent to the summit of the Mount of Olives all the while "weeping as he went; his head covered with ashes and barefoot." What a desert!

David wrote Psalm 63 while he traveled in one of the worst deserts that I can imagine. His son betrayed him, he had to give up the rule of his beloved people, sent the Ark of the Covenant back into the very place where evil was ruling, and fled to the desert. He had lost everything that he held dear: family, anointing of God to rule, and the symbol of God's presence—the Ark. And yet, I want you to turn your heart again to the words of Psalm 63.

What is David's attitude in this Psalm?

_____

_____

Even in the midst of a literal and physical desert, what does David thirst for?

_____

_____

What does he hunger for?

_____

_____

I cannot begin to imagine the hurt and anguish that David's heart must have been experiencing at that moment. Yet, he does not doubt the God that anointed him as king. He does not allow his eyes to focus on the place from which he has fled. He does not accuse God of leaving him or doubt the very goodness of God's nature.

Read verse 5 and enjoy the beauty of it.

He says that his soul will be satisfied as with the richest of foods. He had learned the key to being satisfied in the desert and how to overcome in victory. He had remembered the food that sustains the soul is God and His Word. He knew his God. He had tasted God in the good times enough to remember that He is the richest of foods even in the desert.

Read 2 Samuel 15:30-32, 16:1-2.

Where are they?

_____

_____

What mountain summit are they just beyond (verse 30)?

_____

_____

What used to happen on that summit?

_____

_____

David and his household had climbed the Mount of Olives and had reached the summit "where people used to worship." How hard it must have been to reach that summit and realize the worship was gone. He had not only sent the Ark of the Covenant back into the city, he didn't have a place to worship. He was entering not only a physical and emotional desert; he was entering a spiritual one.

What happened just beyond the summit?

_____

_____

What did they receive?

_____

_____

What was the purpose of those provisions?

_____

_____

I love those words! Isn't it just like God to give us those things to "refresh those who become exhausted in the desert"? Please see that God never sends us into our times of desert without the provisions we need. But, like David, we must realize that God and His words are the richest of foods. He prepares us and He equips us for the deserts so that we can leave those times in the "power of the Holy Spirit."

Read John 18:1.

Where did Jesus and his disciples cross to get to the olive grove?

_____

_____

Read Luke 22:39-48.

What grove was it?

_____

_____

What is happening here?

_____

_____

What is about to happen after this prayer (verse 48)?

_____

_____

Isn't God's Word amazing? I am really sitting here about to burst! It never ceases to amaze me how He is the perfect Author, never leaving out a thing!

Do you see that Jesus and David are in exactly the same place? Note that the similarities go even further than the location. Jesus is about to enter one of the hardest deserts that any person on earth has experienced – the cross.

_____

_____

He crossed the Kidron Valley to the Mount of Olives to pray. He is weeping with such fervent prayer that he is sweating blood. David also is weeping with great lament as he tops the Mount of Olives and leaves the earthly palace and the anointed rule he had been given. Jesus and David both were betrayed by those closest to them. They were hurting and hungering. They both needed to know that their God had not left them. They both could have had their doubts and frustrations at God, but neither did.

Both Jesus and David went a bit further than the summit to accept God's will and His provision. They both knew that God was the only one who could sustain them in their desert times. They knew that their God was good. He Himself would quench their desert thirst.

The very God we love is the richest of all provisions. The acceptance of His goodness and His promise to go with us is all we need to make it in those desert times. Neither David nor Jesus doubted their God. They simply fed on the provision of His promise and His presence.

Take time now to talk to God. He is with you always. He wants to be your provision when you become exhausted in the desert. Let Him be the richest of all foods for your soul. Enjoy the feast!

WEEK 2 - DAY 4: DESIRING THE FLESH

Today begin by inviting God to dwell richly in you. Ask Him to open your heart to Him in a very real way. Ask that He guide your mind and your heart to see Him more.

Read Exodus 16:3.

I know that you are ready to leave this verse, but there is so much groundwork for our study found here. From this verse, we have learned so much about the life that usually is accompanied by a time in the desert. We've learned that we begin to grumble, we forget the blessings of God, we doubt His character, and now—finally—we desire the flesh.

What are the things that the people desired in verse 3?

_____

_____

_____

Why do you think that it was food instead of power, fame, or material possessions?

_____

_____

_____

You see, when we find ourselves in a time of desert, we will begin to look back on the things of the flesh and desire them. No, we may not say that we desire them with our mouths like the Israelite people did, but we sure do think it. We even begin to act on those desires again.

What else are they saying they desire?

_____

_____

_____

Can you believe that statement? "If only we had died by the Lord's hand in Egypt!" Now, these are the very same people who let out shrieks of anguish when they were under the yoke of horrible Egyptian slave drivers. God heard their cry and was moved to the point of rescuing them and performing miracles to proclaim that He was God to them.

They are saying that because of their hunger, they would rather be under the yoke of slavery again and have the food that was given to them in Egypt. Their flesh is crying out to be fed and they are becoming slaves again – to their own flesh this time—instead of enjoying the freedom God provided.

Read Genesis 25:19-34.

What are the two brothers' names?

_____

_____

_____

Who was the oldest and had the birthright?

_____

_____

_____

What did Esau want from his brother, Jacob?

_____

_____

_____

What did Esau have to sell to Jacob for the stew?

_____

_____

_____

What did Esau say that he was about to do?

_____

_____

_____

What amazing parallels in the Word of God! You see, Esau was hungry, just like the Israelite people were. He was sure he was going to die from this hunger, just as the Israelite people thought. So, in the passionate pursuit to satisfy his flesh, Esau sold his birthright, his inheritance. This is the same thing the people of Israel were willing to do. They were ready to pack their bags and head back to Egypt instead of taking hold of the Promised Land that was to be their inheritance as the chosen people of God!

Return once again to Matthew 4:1-4.

What is Jesus' physical state?

_____

_____

_____

What was the "tempter" asking him to do?

_____

_____

_____

Satan was tempting the Son of God when He was hungry. Jesus had been on a 40-day fast and was very hungry. So, Satan looked back at history and saw that when men were hungry they were usually willing to give in to the cry of their flesh and give up their birthright – their inheritance.

So, Jesus and Satan meet in the desert. Satan tempts Jesus to give in to the desires of His flesh and give up the birthright that He has as God the Son. He wants Jesus to be a slave to the flesh and give over the birthright as Esau had done.

What was Jesus' response?

_____

_____

_____

You see, the key to overcoming the flesh in the desert is to cling heart and soul to the Bread of Life. We must realize that even if our circumstances are dry, we are hungry, and our flesh is screaming to be pampered, we must feed day and night on God's Word.

Read 1 John 3:1-3.

Who do these verses say that we are?

_____

_____

_____

Sisters, we are also the children of God! We have a birthright and an inheritance!

_____

_____

_____

What do these verses say our glorious inheritance will be?

_____

_____

_____

Do you see that? It says that our inheritance is to be like Him! That is not all. We will see Him as He is! We will see the Great I AM as He is! I can hardly keep my heart from bursting from my chest! It is a mighty, two-fold inheritance we are given: here on earth, to be like Him, and in heaven, to see Him as He is! This is wonderful news for those who do not give in to the cries of the flesh and sell their birthright.

You see, we will always be children of God. Nothing can change that fact. But we can lose out on the wonderful inheritance that our Father has for us here on earth—in the desert. When we find ourselves in the desert, it is tempting to look to the old flesh and want to satisfy our cravings, but the cost is very dear and very high.

Look back at Genesis 25:34.

Esau ate and drank and then got up and left. We have got to know that fleshly desires are never satisfying. He wasn't satisfied. He gratified the desire of the moment at the expense of the future.

So, Esau despised his birthright. We will never be pleased and filled by feeding on the stew of the flesh. It may taste good for the moment, but later we will despise the fact that we gave up some amazing blessings of God for a taste of stew.

The Israelite people wanted the pots of meat. They wanted the desires of the flesh too. They wanted to gorge themselves to feed the hunger, and that always means going back into bondage. God's Word is our only hope. We must feed on it day and night. We must eat and drink it and when we do, we will be filled. We will be able to live the true life of the children of God. Because in knowing and being filled with Him, we will be like Him!

Take some time now to talk to God about the desire of the flesh you are battling right now. He knows how hard it is. Jesus himself was tempted in the midst of physical hunger. So, He knows how you feel. Lay yourself open and bare before Him and ask Him to give you the strength to battle those desires by feeding on His Word.

WEEK 2 - DAY 5: THE CYCLE OF DISSATISFACTION

Let's begin our time today by asking God to give us ears to hear and hearts open to His Word. Ask Him to meet intimately with you today as we begin. He is faithful to change our hearts and our lives if we only ask Him to.

Read Psalm 78.

Do you see a cycle that has emerged in the lives of the people of Israel?

_____

_____

_____

Explain in your own words the cycle in which Israel has found itself.

_____

_____

_____

What did they always seem to end up doing when things were bad?

_____

_____

_____

What did they do when things were good for them?

_____

_____

_____

It is vital for us to end today with a clear idea that the people of Israel are in much the same cycle of dissatisfaction in which we find ourselves today. They have amazing times with God and He is right before them visually. He is performing miracles and clearing a way for their escape from bondage. He is faithful to every need and want they have.

But the minute things seem like they have gotten hard, the people go back to grumbling again. They are disappointed and ready to turn their backs and go into bondage. They begin to question their God. They want to return to life that is safe and comfortable. The unknown is too hard. Let's just go back to Egypt.

Look closely and ask God to help you examine your own life.

Are you in that same cycle in your own life?

_____

_____

_____

If so, explain how the cycle begins and what you are really hungry for in your life.

_____

_____

_____

We must look closely and allow God to show us the parts of our lives that are caught in the cycle of highs and lows with very little depth. You see, many of us live from event to event, from conference to conference, from Sunday to Sunday. Through the rest of the week we wonder if there is supposed to be more to life in Christ than what we are living. The answer is YES!

Read Hosea 1 and 2.

Who is Hosea?

_____

_____

_____

Who was his wife?

_____

_____

_____

What kind of woman is she?

_____

_____

_____

Who does she represent?

_____

_____

_____

Why did he marry her?

_____

_____

_____

Hosea was a prophet who was commanded by God to marry an adulterous woman in order to symbolize God's love for His people despite their unfaithfulness.

Read Hosea 2:3-8.

This shows us that God leads us into times of desert, slaying us with thirst in order to make us see that we have a need for Him daily. We cannot make it alone in the desert. Many times we look around and notice that we are hungry and thirsty and doubt our loving God. We begin to doubt that He can sustain us, and He must have just been teasing us in those amazing times of refreshment. He must not be able to meet our every need in the times when we need Him most. We doubt He is the One who quenches the deepest thirst.

So, as Gomer and Israel did, we look around and decide to "go after lovers who give me my food and my water" (verse 5). We abandon the God who has parted the waters of our Red Sea and changed our bitter waters into sweetness. Instead we chase after the lovers of this world. We trust the things we can see to satisfy us, and thus we will never experience the true satisfaction of our souls.

Who is the one who provided all along (verses 8-9)?

_____

_____

_____

How do we use what He lavishes on us?

_____

_____

_____

We are caught in the cycle of dissatisfaction because we taste of our God one day and run after the lusts of our flesh the next. We never realize that God is the One who is supplying our needs all along. This world does not offer us anything good. Only God can give good things to us. He lavishes us with blessings even though He knows that after the retreat or conference, we are going to throw His precious blessings at the feet of Baal – this world.

That is our cycle. That is the life we lead day after day. Taking the blessings of God and turning from Him while the food is still in our teeth. Hosea 2 shows us the exact reason why we live life defeated and dissatisfied.

- God makes us like a desert, turning us into a parched land, slaying us with thirst – vs. 3.
- Then, we feel the neediness and turn to the lovers of this earth to supply – vs. 5.
- God does not allow the things of this earth to quench that thirst – vs. 6 & 7.
- We do not realize that all the blessings that we enjoy are from God – vs. 8a.
- We throw His blessings at the feet of Baal, earthly pleasure – vs. 8b.
- We are completely dried out because He takes away our joy and our satisfaction – vs. 9-11
- We do not remember our God and we doubt – vs. 13.

And here many of us are today. We are settling for despair and want. We are living a life dried up and slain with thirst. We forget what kind of God loves us. We try our hardest to make it here on earth until we can be in heaven. We live defeated lives day after day, claiming all the while to be followers of God, children of the King. But, we must read the rest of the story! We must listen with ears of desire instead of despair…

Read verses 14-23.

Oh, sister, isn't that the greatest news! Even though many of us are camping out and wandering in the desert of dissatisfaction today, God is placing us in this thirsty land to turn our hearts to Him. He desires us to live another kind of life in those deserts. One where He will speak tenderly to us and give us back the vineyards and show us the doorway of hope (verses 14-15).

He is calling us out of lives filled with defeat and unfaithfulness to Him. He is calling us to enter into the desert, where we will begin to see His tender love sustain us. He will restore a song to us like the one we had the day we were led out of our captivity from Egypt. It is possible. He is faithful. We do not have to stay in the cycle. We can enter into His vineyard of daily dependence.

Today we must be willing to look honestly at our lives...

Are you living a cyclical life of high and lows?

_____

_____

_____

Are you meeting with God faithfully each day to quench your hunger and thirst?

_____

_____

_____

Do you find yourself thinking of this life as just an enduring time until heaven?

_____

_____

_____

Do you feel you are always living a life of dissatisfaction?

_____

_____

_____

Do you feel that there must be more to the Christian walk?

_____

_____

_____

Do you see others who are walking close to God and desire that for yourself?

_____

_____

_____

Do you wish you could experience the kind of passion you see in other people?

_____

_____

_____

If you find yourself caught in this cycle, let me assure you that God is calling you into the desert experience that could change your life forever. He is luring your heart and desiring to give you all that you could ever want. The key is you must want Him. He is the giver. He is the lover. He is the One we must desire.

Read Hosea 2:19-20.

Sister, if you are willing, God will betroth you to Himself forever. He will betroth you in righteousness, love, and faithfulness. He will bring you into the kind of marriage you could never dream you could have. He will grab your heart so that you will not look the way of the lovers you battle now. He will take this adulterous heart and marry it with the perfect Bridegroom to betroth us in faithfulness and righteousness. Look into the desert, my sister, your Bridegroom awaits!

Take time today to languish in the wonderful love the Bridegroom has for us. Commit today to follow as He lures you into the desert so that He can renew your song – the song of the captive set free!

OUT OF THE TENT

Now that we have been in the desert for a while, we must find out how God intends for us to thrive there. This week will explore practical ways that we can live lives of satisfaction even when circumstances are not what we would choose.

This kind of life will require effort on our part. Like the Israelites, God is calling us out of our tents to gather the provision He has for us to thrive in the desert.

This week's study will be challenging because it will call us out of our lives of mediocrity into lives of purpose and joy. It will take effort on our part to really embrace what God wants to show us in the desert, because our flesh wants to be pampered. We must choose to seek God!

WEEK 3 - DAY 1: REMEMBER YOUR GOD

Today, start your time with God in praise. Focus your whole heart and mind on Him right now. Do not think of all you have to do when you finish. Do not think about those dirty clothes or that messy house. Close your eyes, take a deep breath, and remember your God.

Read Exodus 16:4-6.

What was God going to do to quench the hunger for the Israelites?

_____

_____

_____

What would the provision in the evening do?

_____

_____

_____

When we find ourselves in the cycle of defeat and dissatisfaction in our lives, we must remember who our God is. Our first step is to stop looking to this world to satisfy us and to remember that we have a God who can do more than we could ever hope or imagine. We forget that our God loves us. He is the only One who can rescue us from ourselves.

Read Jonah 1&2.

What came to Jonah?

_____

_____

_____

What was he to do?

_____

_____

_____

What did he do instead?

_____

_____

_____

What happened to him on the way?

_____

_____

_____

What happened to him there?

_____

_____

_____

Jonah is a lot like the Israelite people. We all have a little of that blood circulating around in us to throw the towel in and move back to Egypt when it gets hard. Jonah was commanded to do something he didn't want to do, so he ran away and found himself in the belly of a huge fish. For three whole days he had some things to think about.

Read Jonah 2:1-7.

Jonah is in the belly of a fish and yet he is remembering (verse 7) his God. He has found himself in a watery desert of sorts, but he remembered God. The key to beginning a life of victory and harvest in desert times is to remember that the God you serve is bigger than anything coming against you.

God did this same thing for the Israelite people, by giving them quail in the evenings to remind them that it was He who brought them out of Egypt and He alone who saved them. We are not to look at our surroundings and let them define God for us. Look at God and let Him define our circumstances. He can allow us to begin our times of greatest growth and harvest in the belly of a fish or in the wilderness.

Read Matthew 14:22-33.

Who sent the disciples out onto the sea that night?

_____

_____

_____

Where was Jesus?

_____

_____

_____

What happened to the disciples?

_____

_____

_____

How did Jesus come to them?

_____

_____

_____

Here we are on the rough seas again. Yet this time, it is the disciples who are headed out to sea by Jesus' command. He is praying on the mountain and he sees the disciples fearing for their lives in the storm. Now, to their credit, it must have been a mighty storm because we must remember these were fishermen aboard the boat. They were not novice seamen, yet they were so completely consumed with the turmoil of the storm that they didn't even recognize their teacher.

That happens to us in the desert times. We begin to notice there is less water here than we would like to have. And now that we think about it, hunger is a problem too. And that sun is doing a lot more than tanning our arms and legs – it's sapping our strength and we think we are seeing a mirage. But, sisters, it is Jesus Christ coming to us in our times of trouble. We are just so consumed with ourselves that we don't even recognize Him anymore.

Who tries to walk on the water to Jesus?

_____

_____

_____

Oh, how I love our Lord Jesus! Peter says, "Lord, if it is you, tell me to come to you on the waters." He is still a little shaky and a bit unsure, but he hopes above all else that it is his beloved Master. And our lovely, patient Christ simply says, "Come."

That is our cry. That is the cry from the desert, from the tossing sea, from the belly of a fish. No matter what has you shaky and unsure in this time of your life, Jesus Christ is standing sure–footed on top of those circumstances that have you defeated. He answers the cry of your soul, the cry that says, "If it is You, Lord, please call me to stand where You are, to come and find peace in You, to find victory over the hunger and the waves. I want to recognize You all over again and remember You. Lord, tell me to come to You on the waters of victory."

And He says, "Come."

Take time today to look beyond your circumstances and remember that the God you serve and the Savior who saved you is able to rescue you right now. He is standing in victory today just like He was the day He parted the sea before you. He is holding out His hand and calling you to come on the ride of your life, to surf those waves with faith, to make your desert an oasis, and to turn that fish belly into a limo of thankfulness. You see Him as He really is and remember He is God.

WEEK 3 - DAY 2: REMEMBER THE TEST

Today, start by asking God to meet intimately with you. Give this time to Him and let Him guide your heart and thoughts. We want to be completely in the center of His presence during our time together, so let's invite the God of all wisdom to take over.

Read Exodus 16:4 & 5.

Why did God send the bread from heaven for them?

_____

_____

_____

There is something very important that we must understand here. The Lord has led them by His cloud from captivity to Elim (the refreshing paradise), then to the desert. They have forgotten their God is a loving and saving God. Now He is going to give them what they crave. We may ask why God would pacify such fickle people. Why would He give them what they were whining for after He had already proven Himself?

The answer is that God will test us in those times when we are having our every need met by Him. When we go on those retreats and our spiritual tanks are full to overflowing, the test of God is to see if we will be able to live day by day. It is so easy to feel close to God on the highs of the mountaintops, but we must remember to take what He shows us in those times and live them daily in order to thrive in the deserts of life.

Read Matthew 19:16-24.

Who is talking to Jesus?

_____

_____

_____

What was his financial situation?

_____

_____

_____

What did Jesus say he must do?

_____

_____

_____

What was the man's response?

_____

_____

_____

You see, this man had been given a life of wealth. He had been given times of plenty. But we must also see that this man was trying to live the spiritual life. He had read the commands and kept them. He was probably a star citizen and would have been a deacon in his church. He was not just trying to gain financial wealth when he came to Jesus; he wanted eternal spiritual things too.

Jesus asked him to sell all that he had and follow him. Jesus was extending the invitation to follow alongside him in ministry. Yet, the rich man turned away because he had great wealth with which he was not willing to part.

Are there habits or material things in your life that you have not been willing to give over to God?

_____

_____

_____

What has God blessed you with that you are keeping back for yourself instead of using for His Kingdom?

_____

_____

_____

What we have to understand is that God is a giving God. He blesses us with amazing times of wealth, both spiritually and materially. He gives us not only the desires of our hearts but also the cravings of this flesh in order to test us. He wants to see if we will be faithful with what He is giving us. He wants to make sure that we will live this thing out day after day. He wants to see if we are seeking more than just the gift of God. He wants to see that we are seeking Him.

Read Matthew 25:14-30.

What happened to the servant who was given the most talents?

_____

_____

_____

What happened to the servant with the one talent?

_____

_____

_____

Who was honored?

_____

_____

_____

Who was despised?

_____

_____

_____

This parable of Jesus is showing us that we are given times of plenty so that we will learn to thrive daily in our spiritual lives. We are not to simply bury those blessings in the ground. He gifts us with things we do not deserve because, like the Israelite people, we are fickle. We are chronic grumblers. Yet, in His wisdom and goodness, He gives the unworthy plenty. He gives us much and then He requires much. We cannot think that God will trust us with His plenty when we are daily burying the treasure of God. We take the blessings and then live as if He doesn't exist. Woe to us! He must be glorified in our deserts, and that does not happen in daily defeat.

Do you feel like you are living your Christian walk day after day?

_____

_____

_____

Do you find yourself hoarding the blessings of God and never living beyond the plenty?

_____

_____

_____

Read Philippians 2:6-11.

What did Jesus do with the plenty that God had bestowed on Him?

_____

_____

_____

What did He make himself?

_____

_____

_____

Oh, how we can mediate on those verses. Here we get a glimpse at what Jesus did with all that He had in heaven. He didn't just sit among all that wealth of heaven that is so rightly His. He became obedient to His Father and gave all of that plenty up to become a servant, humbling himself, and being obedient unto death!

What an example of being tested and coming forth as gold! Jesus shows us that when God gives us the blessing of knowing Him intimately, He requires that we live that out daily in the times when there seems to be little. He leads us into the desert and supplies our needs so that we will be faithful to Him daily. This world is looking to see how we live in our deserts. Are we thriving or merely surviving?

Jesus took the cup he did not deserve and brought salvation to us all. He gave us all that he rightfully had in heaven and lived among us as a servant; a servant who did whatever his Father asked, in good times and in bad. Jesus lived out the life here in a desert. This earth was nothing like the comforts of His home. No angelic voices were singing to Him and praising Him. There was no seat of honor right up next to His Father. There was no glory and no honor. Yet, in His faithfulness, He came to dwell among us and give us bread from heaven.

Look closely at how you are living out your day-to-day life. Look to see if your example even comes close to that of Jesus. Most of ours don't. Look deep into Jesus' heart and into the heart of God. We'll see that He desires to bless us, but He requires that we be faithful in daily deserts to what He shows us in plenty. Talk to God and ask Him to tenderly restore your walk to daily dependence. Spend time talking and listening to your Father. He has given you such plenty. Become the faithful servant.

WEEK 3 - DAY 3: POSITIONED FOR HIS GLORY

Today we want to be positioned to see His glory. We want to be looking to see Him come mightily into our lives. Talk to God now and ask Him to turn the eyes of your heart towards Him to see His glory.

Read Exodus 16:9&10.

What did the Israelite people see coming?

_____

_____

_____

Where did they look to see the glory of the Lord?

_____

_____

_____

What was happening while they were looking at the glory of the Lord?

_____

_____

_____

The Israelite people have gotten quite good at grumbling since they have been with Moses and Aaron. They grumbled at the Red Sea, at Marah, and now in the Desert of Sin. They had become chronic grumblers, you might say. Yet, they heard that the Lord was going to supply them with all the meat they could devour in the evenings and the bread of heaven in the mornings. As Aaron got up to deliver another word about their grumbling, the Israelite people "looked toward the desert and there was the glory of the Lord," while Aaron was still talking.

Read Luke 9:28-36.

What is taking place here?

_____

_____

_____

Who is there?

_____

_____

_____

What happened while "Peter was still speaking"?

_____

_____

_____

Notice an important part of the two stories. The glory of the Lord came even while the two men were still speaking. These men were not evil, selfish, oblivious men. No, these were men that God had called to Himself to be used in mighty ways. They were godly men called to lead many, yet neither had positioned himself to see God's glory appearing.

Aaron was giving the people some much needed rebuking. I can see his sweaty face, red from the raging sun, and his weariness of having to always speak for Moses. I can see Him facing the people with determination to deliver a message from the Lord. He begins to notice a far-off look in the people's eyes as they look toward the desert. It is the glory of God appearing even as Aaron speaks.

Now, take a look at Peter. He is on the mountain with Jesus. Before Peter knows it, they are joined by Moses and Elijah! He cannot believe his eyes as Jesus is transfigured before him. He begins to make plans to stay. He is ready to hang curtains and lay carpet. Peter is still talking about how great it will be there forever, when the glory of the Lord envelopes them in a cloud. And it came along as he was still speaking.

How did the Lord's glory manifest itself in both situations?

_____

_____

_____

Where was the glory of the Lord shown to Peter?

_____

_____

_____

Where was the glory of the Lord for the people of Israel shown?

_____

_____

_____

We must notice the glory of the Lord coming in a cloud. His glory has been consistently seen in a cloud. It was there to lead them out of Egypt, through the Red Sea, and to the desert. It was enveloping them on the mountain. We have to know that God's glory does not only lead us and guide us to a closer relationship with Him, but it also envelopes us when we need to have His warm touch. He is not only a far-off wonder in the distant skies. Because of Jesus, He comes and wraps us softly in His glory. We were once far off, but through the blood of Christ, we are enveloped near.

We can also see that God's glory is not only found on our mountain tops. God's glory is not only felt and seen when we are impressed by cool worship leaders and fancy light effects. God's glory is not merely found in the convention centers packed with Christians. His glory is not limited to the retreats that calm our hearts and the conferences that renew our commitments to Him. Oh no! I want us all to see that God's glory is seen at those times and seems to be so thick that we could choke, but that same glory is found looking toward the desert.

Oh yes, in the desert. The Israelite people were not looking up to the mountain, where Moses would soon meet God face to face. They were not looking back at Elim paradise to see His glory. No, they looked toward the desert and saw His glory.

That is it. God's glory is in every time of our lives. In the miracles of the Red Sea, in the bitter times of Marah, the retreats of Elim, the mountain where we see Jesus in a way we have never before, and, praise God alone, in the desert!

Read Psalm 121.

What does the writer do to see his help?

_____

_____

_____

Where does his help come from?

_____

_____

_____

Meditate on verse 5 and 6.

What is God at our right hands?

_____

_____

_____

Oh, how wonderful to read and receive God's precious words. Do you see He is saying that if we position our eyes to see His glory He will be the shade in our desert? He won't let the sun harm us. He will stand so close to our right hand that His presence alone will be all the shade we need from that desert sun.

Sisters, this is where we wipe our sweaty brows, pick up our backpacks and position ourselves to see God's glory. This is where we stop right where we are in our lives and look deep into our desert and see His glory. It is there to behold no matter where we are right now, but we will not see it if we are too busy looking to this world to satisfy us. We will not see it if we do not position our lives in ways that we will see it daily.

Take time right now to be completely silent before God. Let Him reposition your heart. Let His kind hand close your precious mouth and turn your eyes to Him. If you are in the desert, hot and sweaty, look and see that your help is coming. He is coming in a cloud of glory and shade. Look and see Your God.

WEEK 3 - DAY 4: SEEK HIM DAILY

Begin today by finding a place outside to talk to God. Please go out onto your porch, into your backyard, or just sit near a window and spend some wonderful moments praising and talking with God. Look at His creation and praise the Creator. Look at His design and praise the Designer. Just tell God how great He is and invite Him to interrupt your life today.

Read Exodus 16:4-11.

How often were the Israelite people to gather the bread from heaven?

_____

_____

_____

I must tell you that right now I am sitting on a veranda on the most gorgeous spring day in Callaway Gardens. Some high school youth group friends of mine came here to have a girls' weekend together. It has been a time of refreshment and joy as ladies talk, laugh, and testify to God's goodness in their lives.

We stayed up way too late last night sharing our hearts and our lives. We never turned on the TV. We just spent hours giving God glory and praise for what He is doing in our lives and all around this globe. We turned in very late (or early in the morning). The joy of my heart now is that this morning those same ladies, who were testifying to God's grace and goodness, were up despite tired eyes and sleepy heads to meet faithfully with God.

Look back at verse 4.

The Lord was going to rain down the very bread of heaven, and the people were to go out each day and gather enough for that day. You see, we can't simply position ourselves to see God's glory as a one-time event. We can't just meet with God once a week in church and expect that to last all week. No, we must seek Him daily.

We must learn the daily walk with God. We have to learn dependence on Him each morning, when we rise to meet the day. He is there faithfully – are you?

Please read Psalm 1.

What man in blessed?

_____

_____

_____

What does he do?

_____

_____

_____

What is he like?

_____

_____

_____

God begins the book of Psalms by telling us the kind of person that is blessed. I don't know any woman who does not want to be like a tree planted by the streams of life, soaking up the living water, yielding fruit in her season, never withering, always prospering. Who would not want that to be said of her life? Surely I do!

What do those verses say that person does?

_____

_____

_____

The woman who wants to be blessed, bearing fruit, and prosperous must be the same lady who finds herself at the feet of Jesus, being taught every morning. The passage says that she delights herself in God's Word, and on that alone she meditates day and night. It is on her mind and in her heart every day—not just on Sundays, but every day.

We can't expect to be blessed by God when we are never around. We want all that God has to offer us, with none of the commitment. We want to see God produce fruit in us, yet we have not stayed rooted to the True Vine.

_____

_____

_____

Read John 15:1-17.

What must we do to be a fruit-bearing tree?

_____

_____

_____

Who is the True Vine?

_____

_____

_____

Who is the Gardener?

_____

_____

_____

Jesus says that we must remain in Him to bear fruit. He is the True Vine. We cannot be doing our own thing day after day and expect the blessings of God to follow. We will not bear fruit apart from a daily committed relationship with the Vine.

Read John 1:1-2.

What is Jesus here?

_____

_____

_____

You see here that Jesus is the Word made flesh. He is the very Word of God. He is the One we must meditate on day and night in order to bear fruit. The revealed Word of God is also the True Vine.

In my life I was after the external signs of being blessed. I wanted to be prosperous for the Lord, to bear much fruit, and to be solid in my faith. Yet, my delight was in sleeping because I couldn't seem to get up to spend time with God in the mornings. My delight was in my busy day because I could not make time for God. My delight was where I spent most of my day.

This is where the rubber meets the road. We can say with our mouths all day long that we want to remain in Him and bear much fruit. We want the blessings, the external signs without the inward changes. But that is where all the changes must begin – in where we remain day and night.

God led me to these verses. He showed me that not only must we keep our lives from sinful ways (verse 1), we must also delight in His Word and Him daily. Look at the progression here in verse 1. The person at first is simply walking along in the company of the wicked. She looks around and notices that there are some things going on that she probably should not be involved in doing. She is walking with friends that are a bad influence and are making bad choices. But instead of looking to God, she stops a minute or two to hang out for awhile. What could the harm be in just standing around? Then, before she knows it, she is sitting down to join them.

The Hebrew meaning of the word "sit" is like a king to a banquet. She is not only sitting down for a short while, she is sitting down to a feast of mockers of God. But how does this happen?

God is so good to give us the rest of the story of the blessed one. This person does not just keep away from those situations in order to be blessed. No, the true blessing is from a daily delight in God's Word and in His only Son. We can't expect to keep a blessed life of strength and fruit when each day we neglect His Word. We should not think that we will receive the prosperity and abundant life Jesus speaks of when each day we refuse to stop and meditate on Him day and night.

Return to Exodus 16.

The glory of God was to be gathered daily. It was not something that was a one-time event to prove what God could do. It was a lesson in daily dependence for all of us. His glory is waiting like manna with the dew each morning the sun rises on you. The manna of God is found only by those who choose to be faithful daily.

Though we live in times of drought and desert, those who delight in His Word will find that they are planted right by the living waters and producing fruit while others wither. Oh, how that is my prayer for all of us! That we would find ourselves sipping the Living Water, remaining in Him, and bearing much fruit to His glory!

Take some time now to talk to God. Ask Him to give you the desire to meet daily with Him. Tell Him of your faithlessness in areas of your life and ask Him to bring about dependence on Him daily. Then thank Him that even though we are all faithless, He will always be faithful.

May we begin tomorrow gathering God's glory every morning! It is there to be found!

WEEK 3 - DAY 5: GLORY IN THE MORNING!

Please begin today by asking God to open your heart and your mind to Him. His ways are higher than ours. Ask Him to expand your mind and your heart to hear what He has to say. Give over your thoughts and ask Him to focus you. Let's allow Him to pour His living waters into our lives today!

Read Exodus 16:4-14.

What came in the evenings?

_____

_____

_____

What came in the mornings?

_____

_____

_____

God is doing a beautiful thing for the Israelite people here. He is showing them another beautiful facet of Himself. Not only is He the God of miracles, He is but also the God of daily glory. Something else is going on here. Don't skip over the fact that God is telling them that in the morning they will see the glory of the Lord. Just let that rest on you a minute!

Now, I am about to lose many of you right here. Many of you are inwardly groaning right now about the word "morning." There are many of you thinking about just skipping this section because you "are not a morning person." Well, I want to show you through Scripture that we want to be "morning seekers and glory finders." That is the kind of person I want to be too!

Look back at verse 12.

What does it say would happen when they ate the bread?

_____

_____

_____

When would they be filled?

_____

_____

_____

Do you see that? God didn't tell them that they could gather the manna just any time. He said, "In the morning you will be filled." Oh, how we all want to have that in our lives, don't we? In the desert times of our everyday life don't we want to be filled?

Don't you want to enter every day already filled to satisfaction from God and then let the rest of your day be icing on the cake? Wouldn't it be nice to free up all the people in your day just to be themselves and not have to satisfy you or fill you?

I must confess that I am a needy person. I love people and want their love in return. That can make for pretty miserable days. I would enter my day full speed ahead and empty. I had not met with my Father and asked Him to fill me to satisfaction. So I ran ahead into the day just as needy as I could be. I would need all sorts of things from my family and friends. I needed people to be nice all the time to feel full. I needed my husband to listen and treat me like a princess to feel full. I needed my children to act like angels to be full. And I needed my day to go just as planned to feel full. Do you see the neediness?

When God began to show me these verses I was convicted and yet relieved. You see, my husband was not unloving. My friends were really wonderful. My children were a blessing. My day was like everyone else's. I was just eating at the wrong time!

God tells us the remedy for our empty days. He shows us that He will readily fill us every morning with His Bread – Christ, the Bread of Life – who continues filling our lives every minute. He showers down those blessings to fill and satisfy us every morning, and we just sleep right through them!

Have you tuned me out yet? Please keep on reading! It only gets better!

Read Psalm 5:1-3.

When does the Psalmist pray to the Lord?

_____

_____

_____

What does he do in the morning?

_____

_____

_____

What does he do for the rest of the day?

_____

_____

_____

Oh, when God showed me this verse I had a great "AHA" moment! My high school English teacher used to tell us that we could read something over and over again and then one day we would have the "aha" moment! It all came together for me reading these verses.

Here we see that when we seek God in the morning and lay our requests at His feet, we have all day to wait in expectation for what He is going to do! How much more exciting our day becomes! That gives us a little meaning to our day.

You see, God's provision and glory are there every morning. He promises us that! Yet, when we enter our day leaning on our own wisdom, plans, thoughts, and neediness, we will be hungry all day. Yet, God's glory is there to fill us before we ever see our husband's sweet face, our children's sleepy eyes, or head out the door to our workplace. He is there to give us the bread that fills to satisfaction.

He goes on to tell us to lay our requests before Him and spend the day just watching to be amazed by Him. Oh, how that adds a new dimension to our daily grind. When people look at us and notice that we are smiling a little more during our days in the desert, we will know it is because we are waiting for God to reveal how awesome He is! That is the kind of hope a dying world is waiting to have! They aren't asking about the hope we profess, because we are living defeated lives just like they are. We must live counter-cultural lives in order to reach this world for Christ!

We can look at the Israelite people and identify with their neediness. They wanted Moses, Aaron, and God to cater to their every whim and want. We are a little like that too. Yet, in God's goodness He provides a way to be satisfied to completion. We can feast every morning on His manna and be full the rest of the day. The things that used to make us grumble and fuss will just roll off of us because we don't need them to fill us anymore.

Take time now to confess your neediness to God. We all have areas of our lives which we need Him to fill. Ask Him to get you up in the morning so you can seek His glory. Make Him your first priority of the day and watch Him be HUGE the rest of your day. He is that kind of amazing God. He is faithful. Seek Him with all your heart and He will be found! Leave that quail behind and feast on the glory of God!

INTO THE KITCHEN

This week we'll examine the provision of manna that God sent to the Israelite people in their desert journey. It will give us insight into the way God intended for us to live each day of our lives.

A close study of the manna will speak to our lives today. We want to be satisfied and fulfilled each day, but we do not spend time in God's Word. He alone can truly satisfy us in this desert of life. We must begin to turn from what the world has to offer and eat from the feast God has for us each day in His Word.

Enjoy this study of the manna. It has so much to reveal to us about our own lives. Take time in God's Word on your own outside of this study to really hear what God has to speak over you. Eat well!

WEEK 4 - DAY 1: WHAT IS IT?

Begin this time today with prayer. Allow God to refresh and encourage you. Give your burdens over to Him and start this time renewed by His love and forgiveness.

Read Exodus 16:13-15.

What came that evening?

_____

_____

_____

Because the Lord had heard the Israelites' grumbling for the things of Egypt, He sent the quail in the evening. He first sent them something that they knew. He gave them what they desired and craved. Why would He do that?

Has God ever allowed you to have something earthly that you craved?

_____

_____

_____

How did you feel once you received it?

_____

_____

_____

How long did your satisfaction last?

_____

_____

_____

God allowed the people of Israel to have the quail they wanted so badly. It was something earthly they had known and loved. It was comfortable. We crave the familiar and comfortable too. We seem to desire those comfortable things even more when God is calling us to step out on a journey of faith.

That still doesn't answer the question of why God would give them what they desired from Egypt. Why would He even listen and respond to their grumbling?

Read verses 14-15 again.

What came in the morning?

_____

_____

_____

What did they call it?

_____

_____

_____

What did it look like?

_____

_____

_____

What God is doing here is very important. God sent the thing they thought would satisfy them. They had already decided that if God would just send them some quail that their lives would be much better. They craved something earthly in place of something eternal.

God sent the quail first to show them that it would never satisfy them. The things of this earth will never satisfy. God knows this all too well, but it is we who need a reminder every now and again. He wanted them to see how short lived earthly pleasures are. He wanted them to know that the temporal will never outlast eternal satisfaction.

We must see through this that God is able give us what we want. He has all things under His command. But He loves us far more than that. He wants us to know the joy of things eternal—the bread of heaven.

What did the Israelites call the flakes on the desert floor?

_____

_____

_____

What did Moses call them?

_____

_____

_____

The word "manna" literally means in the Hebrew "what is it?" God gave them what they desired first to show them how lacking it would be. He loved them enough to show them that quail would never satisfy them like the bread of God would. They were given something only God could provide. Isn't that just the way God is? We are so content to simply live, and He comes that we may live abundantly! He gives us more than we could ever think or imagine. That's the beauty of manna. It's a God thing!

Take a few moments right now to write down some of the earthly things that you crave.

_____

_____

_____

_____

_____

_____

Would you take time now to give those over to God? Allow God to come and satisfy your deepest cravings with His bread of heaven. It may be hard and uncomfortable. It will take faith and trust in God each day. But the quail of this earth will never quench the hunger of your soul. Only the precious bread of our Lord will quiet the cravings inside.

WEEK 4 - DAY 2: MANNA

Start today off with an open heart to hear from God. Take a few moments to open yourself up to God and what He wants to teach you today. Ask Him to make the Word alive! Seek Him and His wisdom.

Read Exodus 16:16-18.

How much was each person supposed to gather?

_____

_____

_____

These are precious verses. God sends the bread of heaven to His people. Then He tells them to gather as much or as little as they need. Those who gathered much never had too much, and those who gathered little never had too little. That is the kind of math only God could manage!

As women, many times we spend our precious time here on earth comparing how much "manna" we have to how much others have. We look around us and see those who seem to have much more than we have, and we become a little jealous. We look at other ladies who seem to have it all together and wish our "manna" was a little more like theirs. We may begin to think that the "manna" we have gathered is coming up a bit on the short side. We get discouraged that we will never have the kind of spiritual satisfaction that those around us seem to be enjoying.

Read John 6:1-13.

What does Andrew offer Jesus?

_____

_____

_____

Does he think it is enough?

_____

_____

_____

What does Jesus do then?

_____

_____

_____

Many of us have read this story numerous times. We have been taught about the fish and the loaves through the years in Sunday school. But there is a small verse in the story that I never realized.

Read verses 11-13 again.

How much did Jesus give the people?

_____

_____

_____

What does Jesus tell the disciples to do after the people had their fill?

_____

_____

_____

Why?

_____

_____

_____

What did they collect in the baskets—loaves or fish?

_____

_____

_____

Jesus' desire was that nothing would be wasted! He told the disciples to take up the excess barley pieces from the loaves of bread so that not one piece would go to waste. I believe this is why there was always enough for the Israelites. God, in His amazing wisdom, does not waste a thing.

You may look around and feel that others are filled to overflowing with blessings from God while you feel lacking. But God's desire is that nothing will be wasted. Your manna is never too much or too little, because God can and does use everything in our lives. Your desert times are there for a reason. They are to be used for His glory. Are you allowing God's glory to shine through you while you're in your desert time?

Are you allowing Him to take those pieces of yourself that seem to be useless and make them useful?

_____

_____

_____

Do you feel like what God has given you is somehow lacking compared to those around you?

_____

_____

_____

Do you believe that God will always be enough?

_____

_____

_____

Take time right now to think about your life. Think about all the things God has given you, both good and challenging things. God does not allow anything to come into our lives that He can't use. He does not waste a thing. Because we have Christ, the Bread of Heaven, in our lives we do not have to live wasted lives. Spend some time allowing God to show you the power of Christ in each of those areas of your life that seem useless. Let's stop comparing "manna" and begin living lives of purpose!

WEEK 4 - DAY 3: GATHER DAILY

Take time to allow God to speak tenderly to your heart. He is moving and changing you daily to look like Jesus. Thank Him for that. Allow Him to love you and mold you today. Ask Him for guidance as you dive into His Word.

Read Exodus 16:16-18 again today.

Yesterday, we saw that God never wastes anything. We saw that though some of the Israelites gathered much, it was never too much, and when some gathered little, it was never too little. God is always enough.

Today, in these same verses we see another key to living victoriously in the desert of life.

What did the Lord tell the people to do?

_____

_____

_____

The Lord told the people to gather as much manna as they needed. Do you see that God provided the manna, but they had to be the ones to gather it? So many times in our lives we sit around grumbling about our spiritual lives. We see others who seem to have it all together and we grumble. We see ladies who are worshipping the Lord with abandon and we grumble some more. We look around at people who seem satisfied and we grumble still.

God provided the manna; He was faithful. His command to the people was to gather. He didn't ask them to make the manna. He didn't ask them to fully understand the manna. He simply told them to gather it.

Now, remember they had no idea what this stuff was. They had never seen it before. They were told to gather it and it would fill them. That takes some faith.

They were used to the pots of meat in Egypt that they didn't have to work to have. Getting up each morning to gather takes some effort. God wanted them to know that He was faithful to supply the manna each day for them to live and be satisfied to the fullest, but the manna was also sent to test them.

Read Exodus 16:4.

Why did the Lord rain down bread from heaven?

_____

_____

_____

He says that "in this way I will test them to see if they will follow my instructions." He used the manna to test them, to see what was in their hearts. Would they spend their days grumbling and whining, or would they get out and gather the goodness the Lord had sent? Would they spend their time wishing they were back with the Egyptians eating the familiar pots of meat, or would they trust the Lord and eat the unfamiliar?

We are standing at the same decision today in our lives that the Israelites faced each day. Will we get up and gather the manna of God? He has supplied all we need to live in victory and joy each day, no matter what our circumstances look like. We can be fully satisfied every day of our lives, without fail, even in the middle of the driest deserts!

The question is, are we willing to gather? Are we willing to get up each day and live off His Word? Are we willing to put forth the effort to gather as much of God as we need every day? Are we willing to put aside the earthly pleasures of sleep, comfort, and familiarity for the bread of heaven?

Today is the turning point. It is the day of testing. Take today seriously. Stop right now and be real before God. Are you willing to do what it is going to take to live in victory? Please spend time with God right now. Ask Him to help you gather His Word today. Ask Him to show you areas in your life in which you have settled for the familiar instead of victory. Trust Him to lead you to victory one day at a time and then enjoy the manna!

WEEK 4 - DAY 4: TOOLS FOR THE DAY

Start your time praising God for His faithfulness. Open your heart to Him today and allow Him to speak to you. Commit this time to Him.

Read Numbers 11:7-9.

Describe the manna.

_____

_____

_____

What did it taste like?

_____

_____

_____

This is a more detailed explanation of manna than we have in Exodus. In this passage, the people of Israel have been eating the manna for a while. They are tired of the taste and are again longing for the meat of Egypt. They are longing for the things of their old life once again instead of the bread of the Lord.

What are some of the things they did with the manna?

_____

_____

_____

The people didn't just pick up the flakes and eat the manna; they began to use the manna in many different ways. They gathered it, ground it, crushed it, cooked it in a pot, and made it into cakes. It was the staple of their lives. Their lives depended on the manna.

For many of us, we get up on Sundays and go to church. We listen to the Sunday school lesson, sing some songs, and then open our Bibles to hear from the pastor. The rest of the week we do what we want. Then, Sunday comes around and we start over again. Some of us may even open and read our Bibles several times throughout the week and pray at times too. But is God's Word really a staple in our lives?

The people of Israel were so familiar with the manna that they used it in every way they could think of in their daily diets. They didn't just take it and pop it into their mouths; they made it into the very core of every meal.

The first thing the Israelites did with the manna was to gather it. We talked yesterday about the importance and responsibility to gather God's Word, grace, and blessings that are new every day. God is faithful to give us all the things we need to thrive in this desert, but we must get out of our tents and gather them!

The second thing they did with the manna was to grind it in the handmills. The picture here is of two millstones crushing the manna together in order to grind it. The Israelite people would work this manna into a fine powder in order to cook with it. They would work very hard each day to turn the manna into something they could make into many different meals.

In our lives, we must do the same thing with God's Word. It is not enough to simply open our Bibles, read a quick verse or two, and simply go on about our day. We must take that Word and work with it until we can weave it into the fiber of who we are. God's Word must be digested and become part of us. It has so much to teach us that we would be wise not to take it so lightly.

The third thing the Israelites would do with the manna was to bake or boil the manna in pans. The word "bake or boil" here is used to describe a cooking method, but it also means "to allow to ripen." Oh, how glorious God's Word is!

We must be willing to take the time in God's Word to allow it to ripen in our lives. We can't simply flip open the Bible for a minute each day and expect to be satisfied to the fullest. It is a start, but if we never allow God's Word to be ripened in our lives, we won't understand the fullness of His satisfaction in the desert places. When we go to His Word and taste its goodness, we need to let that Word steep in us.

If you have ever cooked, you have known the frustration of waiting for something to boil. You wait. Check the pot. No boil. You busy yourself with another task. Check the pot again. No boil. Wait a minute more. Check the pot. No boil! By now YOU are boiling! You entertain the thought that your pot may never boil.

Then just when you think it might never happen, you see that first precious bubble rise to the surface of your mixture. But you must still wait more. Finally, you have what they call a rolling boil!

Ladies, God's Word takes time to boil in our lives. It doesn't fit into the rapid pace of our lives. It doesn't fit our schedules. It requires us to slow down and wait, but I promise you it will boil. It will become a rolling boil that brings forth good food to our souls. For this to happen, though, it will take patience, time, and effort on your part.

Take a few moments right now to really let God's Word ripen in you. It will take time, so don't get discouraged. Allow Him to show you amazing things in His Word. God's Word is not made for drive-thru service. It is something that must be worked into every area of our lives. Open those areas of your life that need to be soaked in God's Word. Let the Word ripen there and produce a mighty harvest!

WEEK 4 - DAY 5: YOUR MANNA

Today is going to be a little different. We have talked a great deal this week about God's Word dwelling in us. We have seen the ways that the Israelites allowed the manna to become a part of their lives in every way. It had become the staple of their existence, but it took effort on their part to gather, grind, and boil the manna.

I would like you to spend your time today letting God's Word become real to you. I will give you the verses to study, and you make your own notes about what God's Word is teaching you.

Read Exodus 16:19-36.

Take your time. Read the verses slowly and allow God time to ripen His Word in you. Remember that you don't get a rolling boil in a few minutes. Ask the Holy Spirit to teach you. Dig deep. God will supply all you need and bring forth a mighty fruit for you today.

Enjoy this time and be ready to share what God shows you!

NOTES

_____

_____

_____

_____

_____

_____

_____

_____

_____

_____

_____

_____

NOTES

ONTO THE PROMISED LAND

This week is the end of our journey together, but this is a lifelong ride of a lifetime with God. As we close this study, let God speak to your heart. Enjoy Him each day for the rest of your life here in the desert, until you reach the true Promised Land, Heaven.

Though we are strangers on this earth we can live out a testimony of victory here! I look forward to sitting down at the feast of the King with you! We'll have such stories to tell.

WEEK 5 - DAY 1: MANNA MELTS

Spend your first few moments asking God to open up your heart to His Word today and renew your mind. Allow Him time to speak, and be ready to listen.

Read Exodus 16:19-21

What did Moses warn the people NOT to do?

_____

_____

_____

What did they do?

_____

_____

_____

What happened to the manna?

_____

_____

_____

What a visual picture I am getting right now! It's not a pretty one, either. Moses has told the people that they are to gather their manna each morning and use it that day. But some of the people did not trust the Lord's provision, and they gathered more than they could use in one day.

We cannot live a satisfied and victorious life gathering all of our manna on Sundays at church. We think that if we simply come to church during the week and prepare a Sunday school lesson that we are trusting God. But God never intended for us to open our Bibles and be fed by His Word once a week! He designed us to live off of Him every day.

How long do you think you would last if you only drank water and ate food once a week? For a while you might be able to handle it, and even live a fairly undisturbed life. But before long you would lose your energy. You would begin to have health problems, emotional breakdowns, and you would eventually die without a consistent water supply to your body. You would waste away. And to think that we do this to ourselves spiritually!

God designed us to operate at full capacity when our bodies are well hydrated, well fed, and well exercised. Our spiritual lives are no exception to that rule. When we are diving into God's Word and being satisfied daily, we are prepared to do whatever God has planned for us that day. Others begin to notice that while they are wasting away, we are growing stronger.

Have you ever had a time when you felt as though you were wasting away?

_____

_____

_____

During that time, do you remember seeing others who seemed to be growing strong in their spiritual lives?

_____

_____

_____

How did that make you feel?

_____

_____

_____

Read Daniel 1.

What did Daniel resolve not to eat?

_____

_____

_____

What did he eat?

_____

_____

_____

After the 10 days, how did Daniel and his friends compare to the other men?

_____

_____

_____

It's imperative to understand that our daily diet is very important. We must be living daily on God's provision, not on the world's. Not only did God provide for Daniel and his friends physically, but God gave them more knowledge and understanding than any other men around the king. What God gave them was 10 times better than anything the other men could offer.

Desert life is not easy. But what we are eating each day will determine if we will merely survive or if we will thrive. We have a mighty testimony when God sustains our daily life in the desert while those around us live defeated. They are eating from the wrong menu!

You see, the Israelites did not understand about daily dependence on God. God wanted to see what was in their hearts. Would they believe that each and every day He would be the One to provide for their needs? His desire is for us to live off of every Word that comes from His mouth, not on bread alone.

Trusting God is hard sometimes, but it is crucial if we are ever going to stop this cycle of dissatisfaction in our lives. We must wake up each day and find our manna from His Word and trust that He will provide for whatever comes our way. He wants us to trust Him with our very lives each day.

What are some things that you are not able to trust God with right now?

_____

_____

_____

Do you feel like you are wasting away today?

_____

_____

_____

We cannot stockpile God's blessings, just like we cannot gorge ourselves once a week on food and expect that to last until the next week. We were created for a daily relationship with God. Our soul cries out for it, creation declares it, and we won't be satisfied with anything less.

Take time today to look at the things in your life with which you are not trusting God. Lay those things before Him and allow Him to transform them. He is faithful. Trust Him today with your life and meet Him daily to be fed. It is your soul's desire.

WEEK 5 - DAY 2: A DIFFERENT KIND OF DAY

Bow your life to God today. Confess your weaknesses and ask Him to use them for His glory. Take a few moments to lay your life before Him.

Read Exodus 16:22-30.

What were the people supposed to do on the sixth day?

_____

_____

_____

Why?

_____

_____

_____

The sixth day proved to be a different kind of day for the Israelite people. On that day they were commanded to gather a double portion of the manna. It was the only day that God allowed them to keep some of the provision until the next day. It was a day that dawned differently than the rest. It was a day of preparation.

Read John 19.

How precious the Word of God is to us! Do you see that Christ was crucified and taken off the cross to be buried on the 6th day, the Day of Preparation? This was a day on which the Jewish people would prepare to celebrate the Sabbath. The priests were anxious for Jesus to die because it was unlawful for anyone to hang on a cross on the Sabbath day.

Now look back at Exodus 16:22-30.

On the 6th day the Israelites were able to gather a double portion of the manna until the first day of the week. It was their day of preparation for the Sabbath. What does this mean for us today?

The Israelites had to gather a double portion for the Sabbath, but when the Sabbath was over they had to begin gathering the manna again. The manna was incomplete. It was not sufficient for them. Little did they know that the manna was a picture of Jesus. He is the Bread of Life. He is the One who satisfies our hunger and thirst forever. He is manna that never melts away! On that sixth day when Jesus was crucified, we received an infinite portion to satisfy us forever.

Read Ephesians 6:10-20.

What are our feet fitted with (verse 15)?

_____

_____

_____

Your Bible may use the word "readiness" or "preparation." The meaning is the same. Do you see here that our feet are fitted with the preparation that comes from the gospel of peace? That is the gospel of Jesus Christ and the sacrifice He paid for our sins on the cross. We are prepared once and for all if we have accepted Jesus Christ as our Savior.

What are we prepared for, you may ask? And what does any of this have to do with my life today? Hang on. This is where it gets really good!

Our lives in the desert are hard. We grow hungry, thirsty, and tired. You may be thinking that I could never understand the kind of desert you are going through, and you are right. But what I do know is that if we are ever going to break out of this cycle of dissatisfaction and begin to thrive and grow in these deserts, we are going to have to receive God's infinite portion. It will take the supernatural power of Jesus Christ in our lives today!

This is the day of preparation of our study. This is the day when we stop and decide if we are going to trust God and start thriving in this desert of life. Are you willing to take the final steps to freedom?

Jesus Christ is the only way that we are prepared to fight the long battles in life. He is the only One who is going to satisfy us. He is the Word made flesh, God's very own Son. He is the portion that allows us to worship God in the desert. It won't be something we can do alone. It must be a miracle.

You may have accepted Christ into your life a long time ago, but you feel unprepared and defeated daily in your life. Maybe you have never accepted Jesus, and you are simply being driven and tossed each day without direction. Perhaps you are really striving to serve God in your life, but you feel unprepared for the challenges you are facing today. Jesus Christ is the answer for each one of those problems. He is not only enough, he is a double portion, the infinite portion!

Take some time right now to lay your life before God. Confess your needs. Open your heart and allow Christ to be more than enough in your life today. There is nothing too big for Him. If we are going to break out and live a life of complete satisfaction, we are going to need Christ to invade our lives and take over. He prepares us for eternity and the challenges of daily life. He is our manna!

WEEK 5 - DAY 3: RESTING

Take a few minutes before we start and ask the Holy Spirit to open your heart and mind to truth. Ask God to reveal something new to you today. Begin this time with anticipation of what God will do!

Read Exodus 16:29-30.

What did the Lord give the Israelite people?

_____

_____

_____

What were they to do on this day?

_____

_____

_____

Read Genesis 2:1-2.

What did God do on the seventh day?

_____

_____

_____

What else did God do to the seventh day?

_____

_____

_____

Why?

_____

_____

_____

The people of Israel were commanded by God to rest on the seventh day. They did not go out and gather, bake, or boil the manna. They simply rested on that day. But there is something more to this than just taking a break from a busy work week. In the meaning of the Hebrew word "shabbath" there lies something that is critical to our lives.

The word "shabbath" literally means to cease, to stop, or to rest. The Hebrew lexicon goes even further to explain that the idea behind this word is to "sit still."

When was the last time you sat still (not when you were sleeping!)?

_____

_____

_____

When was the last time you sat still and really worshipped God?

_____

_____

_____

In Genesis 2, God rested from the work that He had done creating the world. He didn't stop being involved. He didn't start the earth going and then leave it to its own demise. He also didn't cease to be active as God. None of these are true of the word "shabbath."

God rested in order to enjoy His creation. He takes delight in us and our worship of Him. He loves what He has created and it is very good to Him. You are very good to Him!

A few days ago, I had the opportunity to sit still and just enjoy God. Now, I am an outdoors type of girl. I believe most things can be cured by a little sunshine and fresh air. Both of my little girls were outside playing and I decided to join them. I relaxed into a plastic lawn chair, tilted my face to the warm sunshine, and took God in. I breathed in His presence and enjoyed Him. It was a day I won't soon forget.

That is "shabbath." God gives us times like that to sit still and worship Him. You were created for that purpose. Creation was created to worship Him. All of life exists to worship God and give Him glory. Your body and soul cry out within you to enjoy God. That is what He gave us. What a gift. The gift to enjoy God, the Creator of the universe!

Read Psalm 46.

What does verse 10 tell us to do?

_____

_____

_____

We are told to "be still," but that is not all we are to do. In those times of "shabbath" and resting we are to know that He is God. He gave us time each week to know Him. We must take those times of "shabbath" and really know God through His Word, through prayer, and through celebration.

As we close up this study this week, we have to remember the time of rest in the desert. God is waiting for you to take up your Sabbath rest and enjoy Him in this journey. He enjoys you. His delight is that you know Him as God. Your soul will never know true satisfaction until you have stilled your life enough to really worship and enjoy the God who created you.

Your assignment for tomorrow is to enjoy God. Each of us is created differently. You will surely find that you enjoy God in a completely different way than I do. Please just rest in God. Be still tomorrow and find a place and time to really worship God. Read His Word, pray, and even dance before Him. He loves when His children abandon themselves to Him. Enjoy a "shabbath" even if it's not Sunday!

WEEK 5 - DAY 4: YOUR SHABBATH

Today is your day to rest in the Lord. Below please journal the things that you did and how God blessed you in that time. Perhaps you want to write a prayer or song, draw a picture, write a poem, or simply list your blessings. Whatever you do, enjoy this time and be renewed! I look forward to hearing about it!

WEEK 5 - DAY 5: THE LEGACY YOU LEAVE

Begin your time today thanking God for all His blessings. Ask Him to fill you to overflowing today!

Read Exodus 16:31-36.

What are the people commanded to do with the manna?

_____

_____

_____

Why does God ask them to do this?

_____

_____

_____

The people were commanded to put an omer of manna (one man's portion) into a jar so that future generations could see how God provided for the His people. How beautiful! God not only wanted to take care of His chosen people then, but He wanted them to tell the generations to come of how He had been faithful.

Think about those on whom you have influence in your life. Make a list of those people.

_____

_____

_____

What kind of legacy would you like to leave them to remember you by?

_____

_____

_____

Most of us have someone who looks to us as an example. It may be a husband, child, friend, sibling, family member, or someone younger than us in their faith. We are all interested in the kind of legacy we are leaving on this earth. What does yours look like right now?

_____

_____

_____

God desires that we thrive in hard times. He wants us to trust Him to provide for us and enjoy Him along the journey. But He is also very interested in what we are leaving behind for the next generation. He doesn't bless us so we can hoard those blessings for ourselves. He expects us to take the things He has taught us and that we are learning about Him and pass those on to the people around us.

Who is someone in your life that has had an influence on you?

_____

_____

_____

What was their legacy to you?

_____

_____

_____

Aren't you grateful that God has placed people who left a godly legacy in your life? I am! There have been many people in my life who have strengthened my walk with Christ by their own walk. We must be intentional about the legacy that we leave.

Read verse 34 again.

Where was the manna placed?

_____

_____

_____

What was the Testimony?

_____

_____

_____

Read Exodus 25:10-22.

God commanded that the jar of manna be put before the Testimony so that it might be kept. The Testimony, or ark as found in Exodus 25, is not even created yet! So, what is God trying to say here?

_____

_____

_____

Read Psalm 102:18.

Why were these things written down?

_____

_____

_____

Do you see that God told them to place the manna in the front of the Testimony although it had not been built yet? He is saying that same thing to us today! We are to lay hold of the lessons, blessings, and truths we glean not only for ourselves, but for a generation not yet created to praise the Lord!

God is doing a mighty work in your life right now in order that those behind you may praise the Lord too. You may feel like your desert times are just something to endure. You simply want to make it through alive, but God has other glorious plans for your desert times. He wants to create such an amazing spring of life in you that those not even born will be amazed at what God is doing in your life.

God sees the entire picture. He knew He would tell them how to build a box to house the manna one day. He knew they would have to trust Him on that fact. However, they were faithful to His command even when they didn't understand what He was talking about. Will you be the same?

_____

_____

_____

As we bring this study to a close, I would ask that you treasure the times in the desert. Embrace those moments, because they are precious times in which you can taste God's manna. In the desert, you will eat the bread of angels!

When you come out of your desert in the power of the Holy Spirit, make sure you place that manna in the very front of your testimony. Let God's glory be front row and center. Don't come from the desert believing that you are the one responsible for your own survival. Remember that God's manna was what allowed you to make it through day by day.

God tests us in the desert times. He wants to see if we love Him and trust Him with our lives, families, money, and reputation. He wants us to live on Him and enjoy Him every day. Christ came to be the fulfillment of that manna. He is the true manna. Without Christ we would all be lost, wandering in the desert of sin, and captive to the bondage in our lives. Because we have a God who loves us, He sent His true manna into our camp, and we will eat the bread of angels!

Please savor this verse with me - Exodus 16:35.

Girls, we have come a long way these past few weeks together, but this journey doesn't stop at the end of this study or any other one. We have to break the cycle we've been in and get on with living in victory with God alone! Moving on with God is a lifestyle.

The Israelite people ate the manna for 40 years, until they came to a land that was settled, the Promised Land. We must make our daily diet one of God's life-changing Word. This is our diet from now until we enter into God's glorious home for us in eternity.

Please read Revelation 19:1-10.

What will we eat when we enter into eternity with Christ (verse 9)?

_____

_____

_____

We are invited to eat at the wedding supper of the Lamb! We are chosen to come and feast with Christ! We must hold tight to the testimony of Christ in our lives. We must endure until the wedding feast.

Fellow Israelites, we have come to the end of this study but not the end of the journey. You may see harsh deserts and rocky mountains ahead, but hold tight to the testimony you gain through those times because you have a seat at a feast! I love you and will see you there!

LEADER'S GUIDE

A Note to the Leader

I am so glad that you have chosen to lead this ladies' Bible study! I am looking forward to hearing all God does through this study in the lives of ladies in your community. Please feel free to email me with the stories of God's grace in your lives at desertstories@ desertflowerministries.com.

This study is a challenge to thrive in the deserts of our lives. There are two kinds of deserts in our lives: those we enter into out of sin and rebellion, and those that God leads us into Himself. This study addresses the latter desert. There are times when we find God leading us into places where we do not want to go. We didn't sign up for this! God is gently leading us into these hard times in order to grow us, test us, or to show us His glory and provision in our lives. We will spend the next few weeks finding out how God desires for us to thrive in those deserts.

As a leader, God will call you to be transparent. You may be called to share some things about your own private desert, but in that humility and transparency, God will show Himself glorious! Thank you for being willing to put yourself at the Master's feet and let Him teach you beautiful ways to have your soul satisfied.

Michele Williams, a ladies' Bible study leader for over 8 years, helped me formulate this guide in order to help you get started. This guide is simply a suggestion of how to lead the study. Please adapt it to fit the personality and size of your group. Remember, above all, to yield to the Holy Spirit and how God wants you to lead your group.

Before the Journey Begins...

* Please spend ample time in prayer over the ladies God will bring to the study.
* Study Genesis 15 through Exodus 16. This will give you the entire story from Abraham to the Israelite exodus out of Egypt. Start this study at least a month before you plan to teach. You need a thorough understanding of the context of Exodus 16.
* An important part of this study will be the Oasis groups. These are smaller groups of ladies who will meet together to discuss the week's homework and what God is doing in their lives. These smaller groups allow for more discussion and transparency. They will also serve as accountability and prayer groups.
* If you have a small group, you can serve as both the leader and Oasis Group leader. If you have a large group, you will want to break into groups of about 4-5 ladies.
* Pick a few ladies to serve as your Oasis Group leaders. Oasis groups are an important part of this study. Once you have assigned the ladies an Oasis Group, they will keep that same group the entire study. This will allow for friendships and trust to build. Make sure that the ladies who lead these Oasis Groups are strong spiritually and are familiar with leading groups themselves.
* Meet with your Oasis group leaders to give them their books and allow them time to read Genesis 15 through Exodus 16 also. They must be at least one week ahead of the group they are leading in order to give insight and instruction if necessary.
* Be sure to take ample time to explain the kind of desert we will be traveling through together these next few weeks. It is vital that they understand the synopsis of the study in order to guide their groups. You may encourage your leaders to look over several weeks of the study to get an overall feel for it.
* Pray for your Oasis Group leaders daily and keep them accountable to their study time. They cannot lead where they are not going themselves. Meet again just before your first session to answer any questions and pray together.
* Take time to prepare yourself spiritually. Allow God to speak to you each day in order to have a fresh word from Him for your ladies.

Session 1: Introduction

Leader:

* Prepare your meeting area. I have found that the ladies who take this study thrive in a warm and cozy environment. I try to have the room clean and set up early so

I can spend time getting to know each lady as she arrives. You may want to have some hot tea or coffee ready so they can come in and take a moment to collect themselves from a busy day. Give them a setting in which they feel refreshed, your own oasis in the desert!

* Gather name tags, pens, and books for each lady. It is a good idea to have name tags for the first few weeks until everyone knows each other.

Main Gathering: 30 minutes

* Start promptly to give the ladies the most time in God's Word and in their Oasis groups.
* Introduce yourself and give a short introduction to the study.
* Explain the journey from Abraham to the exodus. It is very important for the ladies to understand the context of this study. Set the stage for Week 1.
* Explain Oasis Groups. Introduce your Oasis Group leaders and break the ladies into groups. You can do this any way that seems best for your group. You can let the ladies divide themselves up or you can mix them up yourself. You choose what works for the dynamics of your group.

Oasis Groups: 45 minutes

* Introduce yourself and allow each member of your group to introduce herself. Allow time for each lady to share her name and why she feels she came to this study.
* Pass around a sheet of paper on which each lady can write her name, address, phone number, birthday, and email address. This will give you a resource to follow up and encourage each lady through the study. Plan to make copies for each lady. This will allow them to contact each other through the study also.
* Discuss the following topics...
  1. What is a desert like? (dry land, empty, wasteland, uncultivated area, etc.)
  2. Name some physical deserts (Sahara Desert, Painted Deserts, etc.)
  3. Name some personal deserts (Job loss, death, anger, depression, etc.)
  4. What does it mean to satisfy? (to meet a desire or need, fulfill, gratify, etc.)
  5. What areas do we need to be satisfied in?
  6. How do we seek satisfaction?
  7. Does the satisfaction we seek, last? (Think hunger...can be satisfied with sugary sweets or veggies.)

* Direct the ladies to the memory verses located past the Leader's Guide section. Ask them to memorize the appropriate verse for this week. Encourage them to be prepared to share this verse in your group next week!
* Ask for prayer requests. Have index cards and pens for the ladies to record prayer requests.
* Pray together.

Main Gathering: 30 minutes
* Leader: call Oasis Groups back to the main meeting area.
* Allow the groups or individuals to share some of their responses to the questions. You may ask your group leaders to share, if the ladies are shy about speaking up at first.
* Make sure each group is on target with the kind of desert we will be studying. Explain that there are certainly deserts that we march ourselves right out into the middle of, but we will be looking at those deserts into which God calls us. Share that our society simply wants to live life with ease and comfort. God does not call us to that kind of life. We are assured in James 1 that we WILL have trials of many kinds. It is important that we are living our lives in the desert with joy! The world is looking to us for the answer to living abundantly. Are we willing to thrive in the desert or simply survive?
* Explain that for best results at getting the most out of the study, do the homework daily.
* Ask for questions and close in prayer together.

Session 2: Week 1: Out of Bondage

Main Gathering:
* This week of study serves two purposes with the same answer. Some ladies in your group may not be Christians, so you will want to be prepared to share the plan of salvation during this time. Use the weekly homework as your guide to sharing the gospel message clearly with the group. Others in your group will be strong Christians. Challenge those ladies to see this week's study as the steps to thriving in the desert. Either circumstance requires the same answer, Jesus Christ. Explain that we cannot be saved from our bondage without crying out to Jesus for help. We cannot do this on our own. We must humble ourselves and ask Jesus to make an amazing way!

* Allow a few moments for anyone to ask questions in the large group about what you have shared. Open the time with prayer together.
* Dismiss the ladies to their Oasis Group.

Oasis Groups:
* Share memory verses.
* Go over each day's homework and ask ladies to share insights from God. Be prepared to lead in your personal insight if ladies are quiet.
* Ask for prayer requests and pray together.

Main Gathering:
* Answer any questions from the Oasis Groups.
* Give a brief introduction to next week's study.
* Ask the following questions to answer or simply to reflect on this week:
  1. How do we get into deserts?
  2. How do we recognize we are in a desert?
  3. How do we feel in the desert?

* Ask if anyone would like to share their memory verse.
* Close the time in prayer.
* Have some time of fellowship where you can talk to some of the ladies personally.

Session 3: Into the Desert

Main Gathering:
* Begin with prayer all together.
* Explain that our goal in this study is to thrive in the deserts of life. We are called to exit these deserts in the power of the Holy Spirit as Jesus did when He was tempted in His desert. If we thrive in the desert, we leave with a mighty testimony that the world is dying to hear. While the world is wasting away, we are thriving! A lost world takes notice of this kind of counter-cultural living.
* Discuss Day 5 and the Cycle of Dissatisfaction. Refer to Hosea 2 and read some of this passage. Make sure everyone understands the cycle we are studying before they go to Oasis Groups.
* Dismiss to Oasis Groups.

Oasis Groups:
* Share memory verses.
* Discuss each day's homework and allow time for ladies to share personal insights from God. Answer any questions.
* Share prayer requests.
* Close in prayer.

Main Gathering:
* Allow some people to share about what God showed them this week. This will help the main group to stay connected.
* Take time to introduce Week 3.
* Ask ladies what they would take to survive in a physical desert. Write these down for next week. Then ask them to make spiritual parallels.
* Close in prayer together.

Session 4: Out of the Tent

Main Gathering:
* Ask the ladies the following questions to begin your time together:
  1. What physical tools for the desert did we talk about last week?
  2. What are some spiritual tools we learned about this week?
  3. If you used the tools, what differences did you see in this week?

* Discuss an overview of this past week's homework. Share what God has shown you so far in your study. Allow them to hear from your heart what God has done in your life.
* Dismiss into Oasis Groups.

Oasis Groups:
* Share memory verses.
* Discuss each day's homework and the insights God gave each lady. Allow time to share about the cycle of dissatisfaction that they are battling right now.
* Share prayer requests.
* Close in prayer.

Main Gathering:
* Ask for anyone who wants to share with the main group. This will keep you connected as a large group.

* Ask the ladies to share what the definition of "enough" is to them.
* Give an overview of "manna."
* Remind them to rely on the Holy Spirit as their guide as they dive into God's Word this week!
* Close in prayer as a group together.

Session 5: Week 4: Into the Kitchen

Main Gathering:
* Use this time to allow the ladies to share about their personal manna time this week. Give them plenty of time to share the insights God gave them. Be prepared to lead this time with your own personal insights.
* Ask your Oasis Group leaders to share their insights also. This will ensure that you do not have silence at the beginning. Get the time started on a high note!
* Dismiss into Oasis Groups.

Oasis Groups:
* Share memory verse.
* Continue sharing this week's homework and insights God has given each of you.
* Share prayer requests.
* Pray together.

Main Gathering:
* Ask ladies to begin thinking about their relationship to God. How do they see this relationship?
* Give an introduction to Week 5, the final week!
* Ask the ladies to think about people who have left a legacy in their lives. Ask them to think of who, what, and how these legacies have impacted their lives. Prepare them to share these legacies next week.
* Close in prayer together.

Session 6 : Week 5: Onto the Promised Land

Main Gathering:
* Take this time to allow the ladies to share about their "Shabbath." Be prepared to begin by sharing about your own time with God. Ask your Oasis Group leaders to have a testimony ready to share. Enjoy this time reflecting on God's goodness.

* Ask ladies to share about the legacies that others have left that have impacted their lives. Begin this time sharing from your own heart and ask the Oasis Group leaders to be prepared to share also. If the ladies are sharing, allow them to go before the Oasis Group leaders. Lead as the Holy Spirit prompts you.
* Dismiss to Oasis Groups.

Oasis Groups:
* Share memory verses.
* Give a little time to continue sharing about the Shabbath and the legacies. Some in your group will share in the small setting instead of the large group.
* Discuss each day's homework and the insights God has given each of you this week.
* This is the final week. Ask for the ladies to share what God has done in their lives throughout this journey. Be prepared to share also.
* Make a plan to keep in touch and keep each other accountable. Don't let this be just another event!
* Share prayer requests.
* Close in prayer.

Main Gathering:
* Encourage time to share with the large group what God has done in each lady's life through this study. Be prepared to lead this time with your own testimony.
* End this time reminding ladies not to let this study be just another study on their shelves. Encourage them to dig deep into the Word of God each day. This journey has just begun! We must be ready to give a testimony of God's provision and glory in our deserts. God desires that we live abundantly in this life. We are called to be a light on a hill; let's not be hidden. Our light can shine even more brightly in the deserts because others want to know how we are able to thrive in hard times.
* Take a few moments to have a dedication time. Play some music or have a time of silence to allow ladies to commit the rest of their lives to God. Give plenty of time for prayer and reflection.
* Close this study in prayer.
* Make plans to follow up with each lady through the Oasis Group leaders.
* Email me at desertstories@desertflowerministries.com and let me know how your study went! I look forward to hearing about what God did in your group! I have enjoyed.

MEMORY VERSES

Week 1

"Jesus answered, 'I am the way and the truth and the life. No one comes to the Father except through me.'"

—John 14:6

Week 2

"O God, you are my God, earnestly I seek you; my soul thirsts for you, my body longs for you, in a dry and weary land where there is no water."

—Psalm 63:1

Week 3

"In the morning, O Lord, you hear my voice; in the morning I lay my requests before you and wait in expectation."

—Psalm 5:3

Week 4

"And when they measured it by the omer, he who gathered much did not have too much, and he who gathered little did not have to little. Each one gathered as much as he needed."

—Exodus 16:18

Week 5

"Blessed are those who are invited to the wedding supper of the Lamb!"

—Revelation 19:9

RESOURCES

Scripture References:

Unless otherwise noted, Scripture quotations are from The Holy Bible, New International Version, copyright 1973,1978, 1984 by International Bible Society.

Scripture quotations marked NLT are from the New Living Translation.

Other resources used:

Spiros Zodhiates et al.,eds.,The Complete Word Study Dictionary: Old Testament (Chattanooga, TN: AMG Publishers, 1992).

James Strong, Strong's Exhaustive Concordance of the Bible (Nashville, TN: Abingdon Press, 1970).

LaVergne, TN USA
02 March 2011
218445LV00002B/69-108/A